WAR & GRACE

War & Grace

ISBN: 978-955-44416-0-6

Fourth Edition

Scripture quotations are from the *New Kings James Version* unless otherwise specified.

Cover design by: www.ideeal.de
Typesetting, editing and layout: Jeremy Muller
Printed in Sri Lanka by: The Print Shop

WAR & GRACE

The Life & Ministry of Dr. Verghese Chandy

Acknowledgements

I am thankful to Hildegard, my wife and companion, for the encouragement she has been to me to write this book. She has recalled details of many incidents and placed them in the proper time line, having studied the manuscript methodically.

I am most grateful to Jeremy Muller whose professional expertise was of paramount importance in editing and proof-reading. I also appreciate his technical assistance in compiling this book. Ranjan Joseph's support in editing is also appreciated.

Dedication

To my sons, Mark, Stephan and Dennis.

They have been an integral part of our lives as we lived through the winter of the turbulent years in Sri Lanka, the exciting Springtide in Germany and the peaceful summer days in America.

We thank God for every remembrance of them.

"It was breathtaking... a tower of strength."
F. M. – Negombo, Sri Lanka

"It is a faith builder..."
B. C. – Trincomalee, Sri Lanka

"I read the book three times and am inspired to do more for Christ."
R. M. – Batticaloa, Sri Lanka

"I have never read a book which had such an impact one me."
Student – Colombo, Sri Lanka

"It will be standard reference for the next generation."
D. B. – Bangalore, India

"I read the book in one sitting."
R.K. – Colombo, Sri Lanka

"It illustrates how unbelievable challenges can be overcome by the Grace of God..."
G. K. – Germany

"When I finished the book, tears were tolling down my cheeks when I realized how much the island nation had suffered, yet was sustained by the *Grace of God!*"
H. C. – Singapore

It gives me great pleasure to recommend the book "*War & Grace*" written by Dr. Verghese Chandy. I have been a close friend of his parents for many years especially his father M. M. Chandy, who was an evangelist.

I remember the early days when young men from the Bethesda Gospel Hall were seeking the baptism of the Holy Spirit and he was one among them. From that time his ministry has had a significant impact on the Body of Christ.

Pastor Chandy has remained resolute and unwavering to his calling and this has brought renewal and restoration to many churches.

I trust that this book "*War & Grace*" containing narratives of inspiring events, will challenge its readers to serve the Lord more courageously.

***Rev. Dr. Colton Wickremeratne** – Senior Pastor (emeritus), Peoples' Church, Assembly of God, Sri Lanka*

It is with great pleasure and spiritual benefit that I have read this book. It is a masterful blend of great spiritual happenings and very practical human developments. Dr. Chandy has an eye for the beauty of nature and a heart for the suffering of mankind. His kingdom-vision is legendary and his perseverance deeply inspiring. He sketches in captivating manner the broad outline, without losing sight of the important details. A treat to read!

***Dr. Herbert Ros** – Volksmission (The People's Church), Stuttgart, Germany*

A challenging book for young people interested in Ministry.

***Ranjit De Silva, Ph.D.** – Empowered Leaders One, Sri Lanka*

Pastor Dr. Verghese Chandy is my mentor, held in high esteem and regard in the Lord. God brought a group of young people to Bethesda Gospel Hall with a divine mission and purpose in the Kingdom of God. Bro. Chandy mentored and galvanised us in our faith with his love and impartation of the Word of God. His dedicated ministry in Sri Lanka for over 50 years has ushered in over 50,000 people to the Kingdom of God, raised up powerful Pastors and birthed new Churches. He is an Apostle, worthy of recognition. I commend this book to inspire many to take up a similar challenge.

***Sam Rajendran** – 10 Georgia Place, The Keys, Keysborough 3173, Australia*

The inspiring and awesome narrative of the life and ministry of Dr. Verghese Chandy is a living testimony to the fact that the 'Acts of the Holy Spirit' are yet to be finished! Not unlike the apostles of old, he has endured many hardships, encountered numerous dangers – and experienced amazing spiritual victories. While the search for the power of the Spirit and the winning of men and women for Christ has been the driving force behind Dr. Chandy's mission, he has also cared deeply for the poor, marginalized, and vulnerable. This book will be a great source of inspiration and blessing for leaders and ministers, as well as every Christian interested in the mission of the Spirit in the world.

***Veli-Matti Kärkkäinen** – Professor of Systematic Theology, Fuller Theological Seminary, Pasadena, CA, USA*

FOREWORD

Dr. Yonggi Cho is pastor of the largest church in the world in Korea with one million members and has sent this recommendation.

I would like to recommend the new and exciting book written by Pastor Verghese Chandy of Colombo, Sri Lanka. This book will educate the reader and inspire him or her to greater heights of faith, hope and trust in our blessed Lord Jesus Christ.

It is entitled "War & Grace", and it is a true account of the thirty-year war in Sri Lanka, and how the Lord moved mightily on behalf of His beloved people. This book reveals the miraculous manner in which The Lord Jesus Christ built His Church through the mighty power of The Holy Spirit.

I have known Pastor Verghese Chandy since 1974, when I met him in Seoul, Korea. He is a faithful man of God and minister of The Word of God. His ministry at the New Covenant Church in Colombo verifies and confirms his life and work as being greatly fruitful and blessed.

Please read Pastor Chandy's new book and be renewed and transformed by the glorious Holy Spirit power and the inspiration of our Lord Jesus Christ. It is a wonderful Word of Testimony demonstrating what God can do.

Sincerely and in His love,

Yonggi Cho
Church Growth International
Chairman of the Board

INTRODUCTION

The front cover captures most of the sentiments expressed inside.

The sword is a pictogram, of man's violence and animosity against each other. The Cross, the symbol of love and mercy.

The book narrates some of the events that shook the island nation and plunged it into chaos.

The artist picks up the offending sword and drives it into the ground. It is then transformed into a cross, and a crown of thorns hangs on it. The cross of Jesus and the crown of thorns declare that there is forgiveness and reconciliation for all. This is the story of War and Grace.

While war was raging in the island, the Grace of God appeared and brought peace and hope to many, at the most unforeseen moments.

The spiritual renewals, the rebirth of churches, the equipping of future ministers, the tranformation of multitudes at crusades and camps were abundant evidence that the Grace of God was ever-present at the gravest hour.

Our prayer is that, "we shall cherish the old rugged cross and exchange it someday for a crown".

SRI LANKA

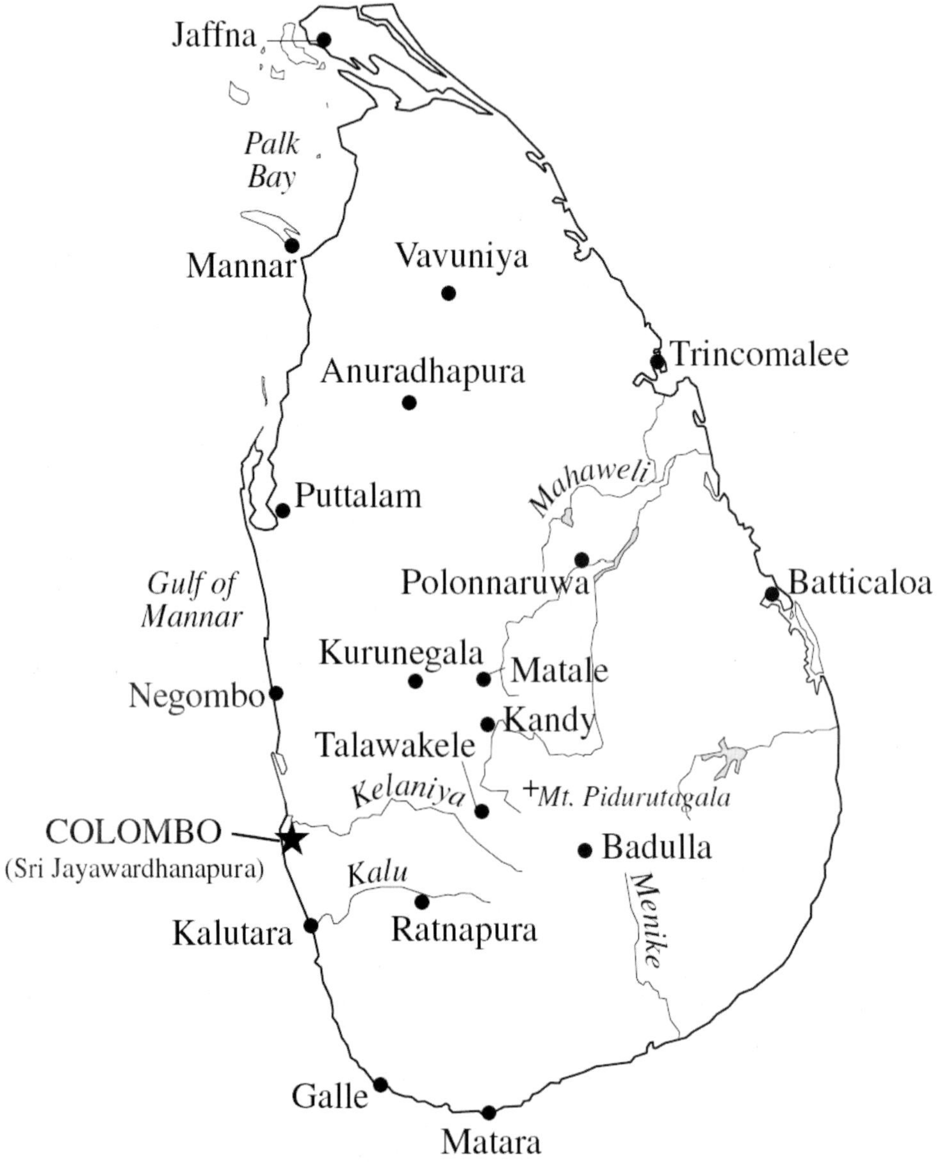
Jaffna
Palk
Bay
Mannar
Vavuniya
Trincomalee
Anuradhapura
Mahaweli
Puttalam
Polonnaruwa
Batticaloa
Gulf of
Mannar
Kurunegala
Matale
Negombo
Kandy
Talawakele
Kelaniya
+Mt. Pidurutagala
COLOMBO
(Sri Jayawardhanapura)
Badulla
Kalu
Menike
Kalutara
Ratnapura
Galle
Matara

1

My Visit to Jaffna. A Change of Travel Plans. Riding the Yal Devi. The Human Bomb Locator. Dedication of the Zion Church. The Pallai Train Robbery. The Journey Home.

THE YEAR WAS 1985 AND I HAD RECEIVED AN INVITATION TO dedicate the Church in Jaffna, the capital city of the Northern Province.

Jaffna, also called *Yapanaya* by the Sinhalese and *Yalpanam* by the Tamils, was not, at that period in this island's history, the most popular destination. Since the 1980s, insurgent uprising, military occupation, extensive damage and ruin, expulsion and depopulation had come about. Life in this part of Sri Lanka hung by a thread as the struggle for supremacy between the separatists and military indiscriminately claimed the lives of many innocent bystanders.

In 1989, at the peak of the separatist war, many feared to travel to the north, and just as many would question the wisdom of such a journey. Yet the faithful had persevered and, by faith, erected the building that would house God's church in that area and its dedication was a priority.

The Tamil people of Jaffna were predominantly Hindu, with a smattering of Moors and Muslims, and there was a small but influential number of Protestants belonging to the Church of South India, the successor organisation of the American Ceylon Mission and other colonial era Protestant churches.

The dedication of the Zion Church would be on a Sunday, and Saturday morning found me leaving the hill city of Kandy where I lived, to Colombo,

Sri Lanka's commercial capital on the west coast, where I would take an air-conditioned bus to Jaffna. The journey to Colombo was uneventful and I had already resigned myself to the rest of the day's long journey.

Reaching Colombo mid-morning, I walked to the Jaffna bus stand, pre-paid ticket in hand, when something prompted me to take the train instead. This change in travel plans made no sense. I had already paid for the journey which would take me all the way to Jaffna town, whilst the train, due to the conflict in the north, only ran up to Pallai, twenty kilometres away from Jaffna town, and I would have to purchase another ticket. Nevertheless, with fresh ticket in hand, I boarded the comfortable *Yal Devi,* an intercity express train that connected the capital to the northern cities.

The *Yal Devi* ran twice a day from Colombo to Jaffna and was commissioned to connect Colombo, Jaffna and Kankesanturai. It rumbled on the track for decades until the separatists destroyed part of the track as they believed that this train brought the people of the north and south together, which was against their policy.

The name *Yal Devi* has become part of the Jaffna Tamil language. When a person walked fast, people would say 'he (or she) moves like the *Yal Devi*'. Before the destruction of the track, the people of Jaffna loved this train because it was their link to Colombo and the outside world. Crowds gathered to greet their families and friends, and porters and taxi drivers competed for business from the affluent passengers from Colombo. The moment the train arrived at the Jaffna station, word would spread that the *Yal Devi* had arrived. There were even some residents who would not go to sleep until the arrival of the *Yal Devi.*

Settling into my seat, I made myself comfortable. A short while later I heard the sharp blow of the station master's whistle, signalling the commencement of the journey to the north. I looked on as the landscape shifted from commercial Colombo to greener suburban areas and towards the cooler and higher elevation of the hill country. The train halted at a few stations on the way, bypassing Kandy and took a circuitous route through Kurunegala. From Kurunegala, it was a flat terrain and the train chugged by verdant paddy fields where farmers were tilling, sowing or harvesting the golden grain. As it proceeded further north, the terrain became more barren and sparsely populated except for paddy fields and pastures where cows were grazing in the open. It was not uncommon for the *Yal Devi* to slam broadside into elephants that would cross the rails at night, flinging them onto the side of the track.

The rail track crossed the Chundikkulam Lagoon, also known as the Elephant Pass Lagoon, and into the Jaffna Peninsula to reach Pallai soon after. This was the end of my journey by rail, as the *Yal Devi* would go no further.

The city of Jaffna was still a good twenty kilometres away and I took a bus the rest of the way. Here I finally was: Jaffna. It had been a tiring journey, yet it was not quite over. At the station to meet me was Pastor Josiah, a slim, tall man of fair complexion and meticulously dressed. He was there to greet me, and provide me with the last leg of my journey to the hotel…riding as passenger, with luggage and all, on his bicycle!

Josiah pedalled me all the way to the Palm Garden Hotel in the city where I checked in. This once popular hotel was completely empty of guests and most of its staff, with only the cook and receptionist in attendance.

"Do not be afraid if you here gunfire at night," said Josiah. He had a manner of speaking which was crisp, clear and confident. I told him not to worry, that I wouldn't be.

The evening had drawn on and it was now past dinner hour. I went to the dimly-lit reception and inquired after the bus which had left for Jaffna from Colombo that morning. The receptionist told me the bus had not yet arrived and after he made a few calls, found out that the bus was waylaid in Kurunegala and several people had been killed. The very same bus I would have been on if I didn't alter my travel plans! I thank the Lord who had prompted me to switch from the bus to the train that day.

Retiring to my room, I slept fitfully until I was woken to the sound of distant gunfire and explosions. I glanced at my watch. It was 11 pm. I prayed and tried to get back to sleep. A while later, the '*BOOM*' of distant explosions began again and kept on at intermittent intervals. I finally gave up on getting any sleep and at 1:30, I walked down to the reception where I found the cook on duty. The sound of gunfire, which I had first heard in the distance, was getting undeniably closer to the hotel.

As I stood there, I heard the resonating blast of another explosion. The cook looked up and observed: "That's in Gurunagar!" Astonishing! The man was so used to the sound of explosions that he could identify where each blast originated from! Another '*boom*' was heard, this time from another direction. The cook pricked up his ears. "That's in Karainagar!" he proclaimed. I was in the presence of a Human Bomb Locator! At the next sound of an explosion, sure enough, he piped up: "That's in Thirunagar!"

Comforted with the fact I had a man of such calibre on guard, I retired to my room once more, although I hardly slept the rest of that night and found myself longing for daybreak.

The dedication service was to begin at 9.30 that Sunday morning. The hotel was close to the church, which was situated in the heart of the town surrounded by markets and shops. Pastor Josiah sent a brother from the Church who came to the hotel, once again on a bicycle. He came bearing the appalling news that we couldn't leave for the Church as the LTTE[1] had killed several people and their bodies were lying in the street. We would have to wait till the dead were removed. There was little else that I could do but get myself ready and wait in the foyer for the brothers to come and collect me once it was clear to go outside.

When we finally left for the church, I passed through a town that was deserted. Shops were closed, vendors afraid to open their doors. The service eventually began at eleven o'clock that morning when people began to trickle in through the church doors. Many believers had had to walk long distances to come into town as there was a mere smattering of buses plying their routes. What courage and commitment! What a testimony that these men, women and children would brave the dangers of their surroundings to worship at the house of the Lord!

The church structure itself was unusual in its build, unlike other typical church buildings by comparison. The main hall was flanked by two large balconies that overlooked the hall and could seat maybe about 350 parishioners in all.

I was welcomed by the presiding pastor and then walked up to the pulpit. I preached from the Book of Haggai with the message centering on the proclamation that "The glory of this latter house shall be greater

[1] The Liberation Tigers of Tamil Eelam, commonly known as the LTTE or the Tamil Tigers, a separatist militant organization that was based in northern Sri Lanka

than of the former," *(Haggai 2:9 – KJV)* all the while hearing the sound of distant gunfire and explosions.

And there it was. God's work was being done. A church had been dedicated; it's believers joyous despite being in the midst of conflict and slaughter, their hearts brimming with hope and faith. The very act of building a church would have been a tremendous act of faith as one ill-aimed bomb would bring it all crumbling down. This was the beginning of the Zion Church in Jaffna.

Josiah took me to his house where I shared a meal with his family and then returned with him to my hotel. He suggested I remain a few days, "at least stay on till Wednesday," he said, but I insisted that I should return to Kandy as soon as possible.

The next day they made sure I got a bus that would take me to Pallai to catch the 1.30 train leaving to Colombo. It was a Monday, yet there was hardly any traffic on the road. The bus was packed with passengers, most of them, like me, going to catch the afternoon train. The passengers were all squeezed in like sardines in a can and were constantly thrown against each other as the bus rocked over the badly damaged and pot-holed road.

The bus drove by verdant, green paddy fields. There were a few farmers at work in the fields and several cows were grazing in their pastures. The grass was brown as there had been no rain for some months. Except for a few bullock carts and bicycles, we passed very little traffic. The bus stopped in front of the Pallai station at about 1.00 in the afternoon. There was a mad scramble of people pushing and shoving to get off the bus. I went up to the station counter and bought a ticket to Kurunegala, from where I would take another bus to Kandy. The *Yal Devi* was on the track. People were getting on to the train and compartments were filling up.

I sat next to a window facing the Railway Station, just a few compartments behind the engine. The air was dry and hot, not unlike Colombo. The seats in front were all occupied and those who came later had to make do standing in the aisle. I glanced at my wristwatch. It was a quarter past one. The train was scheduled to leave at half past.

Suddenly I realized that those in front of me were craning their necks and peering out the window. Those in the aisle started forward, leaning towards the windows to also try to catch a glimpse of some commotion outside. As I stretched out my neck to see what was going on I saw a dark swarthy figure dressed in white sarong and shirt running past me. He was panting and carrying a rifle. I literally felt him brushing past me as he ran towards the end of the train where the guard room was located. As he flew by, I could see through the large long windows of the ticket counters, three armed men. One pulled out a drawer containing the collection of the day and the other held a large sack for the money to be poured in. As the next drawer was pulled out both the cashiers backed completely away, looking on in fear. Tying up the two sacks, they fled the station; the other passengers in my compartment holding their breath. They disappeared from sight and seconds later I heard the screech of tires and they were gone.

It was now twenty-five minutes past one. In just ten minutes, the group of young men, who we found out later were LTTE cadres, had covered the guard room and whisked away the entire collection of the day.

The Station Master stepped out onto the platform. He was clad in white trousers and long sleeved shirt. In his hand he held a whistle and he stood there, face drawn and serious, arm raised to blow his whistle. Our eyes met and I shook my head at him trying to convey my unspoken sympathy. He understood and nodded back at me as if to say "what could I do?"

He blew the whistle and the *Yal Devi* responded with her own loud '*TOOT!*' With a clang of couplings and a soft pull, we began moving forward and gaining speed. The passengers went back to their seats, no one uttering a word, looking at each other in shock and disbelief. If someone had an inkling of what would happen and had tipped off the army, they would have tried to ambush the young rogues which would most certainly have resulted in a gun battle.

I was certainly glad when the train left the station; glad that I was on my way back home.

At Kurunegala I disembarked and found a bus leaving for Kandy which was about one hour away. It was past eight in the evening now and the bus was full of passengers. Halfway to Kandy, smoke began to bellow out of the engine and there was a stampede to get out of the bus. Not taking any chances, I threw my bag out of the window and squeezed past the other passengers who were struggling to make headway, dragging their luggage with them. Moments later, just as everyone had gotten clear of what many thought was an imminent fire or explosion, the conductor announced that they had fixed the problem and we had nothing to worry about.

The bus revved up its engines again and the last leg of my journey back home began. I reached home safely that night and related my adventures to the rest of the family. I retired that night thanking the Lord for his protection on the trip to Jaffna.

2

The Clouds of War. Exodus to Maramon, the Place of My Birth. The Maramon Convention. My First Glimpse of the Sahibs. Return to Ceylon. The Malayalam Mission.

MY CALLING HAS TAKEN ME ACROSS THE GLOBE, EVANGELISING, preaching the gospel, praying for and ministering to groups and individuals, pastoring and mentoring, teaching and healing, building churches, and through it all, witnessing the innumerable and incredible miracles God has performed. My journey to Jaffna highlights a few dominant traits that run through the rest of my story. I will name these traits; some being good while others not so much. I have, in my life, lived through ethnic strife, war and conflict, mistrust, deceit and desperation, yet I have also experienced miracles, divine intervention, the dedication and the courage of God's servants and His presence in my life and ministry every step of the way. I have seen God opening doors where they were previously sealed shut and despite all the works of evil men and demonic forces, witnessed innumerable times the mighty delivering hand of God.

And to all this there was a beginning, a time when my life and story really began. There are family and friends, influences and revelations, experiences, both good and bad that have moulded me into the man, husband, father and pastor I have become. Retrospectively, I can look back and see how the hand of God had guided me throughout my life and ultimately, to Him I give all glory and honour and praise. So this is my story and what better place to begin than at the very beginning.

* * *

It was the year 1939. War clouds were on the horizon both in Sri Lanka (then known as Ceylon) and abroad. Whilst Britain and France declared war on Germany, two days after Germany's invasion of Poland, heralding the start of the Second World War, political ethnic tension was also rising in Ceylon, festering into the first Sinhala-Tamil riots.[1]

My father, M. M. Chandy, who was attached to the Good Shepherd Church in Colombo, decided to take our family back to my mother's ancestral home in Maramon, Tiruvella in the southern Indian State of Kerala. It was in Maramon where I was born and raised for the first seven years of my life.

Tiruvella is considered to be the heart of the Mar Thoma Syrian Church of Malabar which was the largest Christian community in India. The town of Maramon is recognized as a centre of Christian culture and influence throughout India. Maramon is also famous as the birthplace of 'Palakunnathu' Abraham Malpan[2], who was leader of the reformation in the Syrian Church of Malabar in the 19th century[3]. This church was founded by St. Thomas, one of the Apostles of Jesus Christ, in 51 AD.

The Maramon Convention was the largest assembly of Christians to be held in India for over a century. It was held in February of each year on the vast sand bed of the river Pampa near the Kozencherry Bridge. Kozencherry is also the birthplace of my father, M. M. Chandy.

A giant tent or *pandal* was raised, seating over 160,000 people with a tithe convention ending on the last day of Lent. Attendees would sit on the dry sandy river bed and the elderly and weak were given chairs to sit on. A smaller tent was also erected next to the larger one for people with infants and children below five.

I remember my mother taking me to this convention and as we walked along the white sands of the river, my mother pointed out two men walking towards the *pandal*. They were neatly dressed in grey suits and carried Bibles with them. My mother told me they were the *Sahibs* (Europeans).

---

[1] *Ref:* Dr. Jane Russell. (1982) *"Communal Politics under the Donoughmore constitution."* Tsiisara Prakasakyo, Dehivala.

[2] *Malpan* means 'teacher'.

[3] *Ref:* Zac Varghese & Mathew A. Kallumpram. (2003). *"Glimpses of Mar Thoma Church History."* pp. 28-33.

It was my first glimpse of European missionaries.

In 1946, we returned to Ceylon, travelling over 350 kilometres by train from Pathanamthitta. Across a barren and sandy wilderness, we crossed the Pamban Railway Bridge to arrive at Dhanushkodi, a town at the southern tip of the island of Rameswaram. Here we faced the crowds at the Quarantine Office where they checked us for cholera and smallpox, and then the wait for the ferry that would take us across the Palk Bay to Talaimannar. This popular ferry service operated until 1964, when a cyclone ripped through, completely destroying Dhanushkodi, just as a train was about to enter the station. The track and pier were heavily damaged and the town of Dhanushkodi was never rebuilt; the ruins of the station and railway track remaining untouched to this day and Dhanushkodi remains a ghost town. In 1982, a small ferry service once again began operating, but was closed down due to the conflict between the Sri Lankan military and the LTTE.

The long wait for the ferry made one thirsty. The water tasted of salt and was almost undrinkable but there were plenty of juicy oranges to be bought from vendors who were selling it to hundreds of thirsty passengers.

Finally, the ferry arrived and after the to-be-expected rush to board, our journey across the Palk Bay began. To our south was the partially submerged ancient land bridge, the Setubandhanam, which geologists believe once connected Sri Lankan and India. This 'bridge' was also known as the *Rama Setu* or Rama's Bridge harkening to the Sanskrit legend of Rama and Sita and the ape men who supposedly built this bridge[4]. In 1804, a British cartographer called the stretch of limestone shoals Adam's Bridge, probably referring to the Abrahamic legend of Adam who, it is said, crossed into Sri Lanka over this bridge and climbed the island's tallest peak (Adam's Peak), where he stood repentant on one foot for a thousand years, leaving a large hollow mark at the mountain's peak resembling a footprint[5].

We boarded the train which left Talaimanner in the evening and journeyed throughout the night to arrive at the Colombo Fort Station in

---

[4] *Ref:* Adrian Room (2006). *"Placenames of the World."* McFarland & Company. p. 19. ISBN 0-7864-2248-3.

[5] *Ref:* "Adam's bridge". *Encyclopædia Britannica.* 2007

the morning. All passengers who returned to Sri Lanka had to present themselves at the Quarantine Office at Fort for more medical checkups to determine whether they had contracted cholera or small pox.

My father, mother and I arrived at the house of Rev. C. C. I. Abraham, the Priest in Charge of the Malayalam Mission. My father was the Catechist/Pastor of the congregation.

The Malayalam Mission was one of its kind and was established by Bishop Cecil Horsley of the Church of Ceylon[6]. The members were expatriates from Kerala who traced their origin to the Syrian Christian community. Its members were teachers, accountants, and people who worked in various offices in Colombo. Bishop Horsley himself became Bishop of Gibraltar a year later and eventually breathed his last in March of 1953.

The Good Shepherd Church was situated down Jawatte Road in Thimbirigasyaya. Sundays would see him leave our home in Swarna Road earlier than the rest while we, a while later, would take the bus from *Redi Mōla* (Weaving Mills) and get down at Thimbirigasyaya Junction where we walked the short remaining distance to church.

The sexton, Coilpillai, would ring the huge church bell twice. The first ring ten minutes before the commencement of the service and then once again, sharp at eight o'clock. The bell could be heard a mile away. None of us owned a wristwatch and the earlier bell compelled us to walk faster if we were getting late. The services were liturgical which included singing of both hymns and songs. There was sermon preached alternatively by the Priest and my father, who were both, during the service, attired in priest's robes. During the years I attended the church, a man that always sticks out in my memory was Mr. Lazarus, who faithfully played the organ and led the singing. Always dressed in white national dress, his strong baritone voice is one that I will never forget.

I remember Rev. Abraham officiating at the baptism of my brothers Libertus, Jacob and my sister Roshan in the church. There was a baptismal pond where children were baptized according to the Anglican tradition. They had some members standing by as godfathers and godmothers, who took on the responsibility to pray for and encourage them to grow in faith.

---

[6] *Ref: "The Ceylon Liturgy"*

Good Friday services would last up to three hours which I found long and uncomfortable sitting on the wooden pews. Later, the time was reduced to two hours and the sermons shorter. The messages would centre on the seven words Jesus spoke from the cross.

The Anglican Church calendar is structured around the major events in the life of Jesus Christ: Christmas, Lent, Holy Week, Good Friday, Easter, Pentecost, the Ascension and Advent. These events helped the congregation spend time in self-examination during Lent, remember the passion and death of Christ, the glorious resurrection and the advent of the Holy Spirit, then Advent and on to Christmas. The church was enriched by the remembrances of these great events and helped parishioners get a robust understanding of the Faith. In contrast, we, today, witness churches that continue to teach and preach just a few pet doctrines and deprive the Body of vital teaching necessary for a robust living.

3

Reverend Linguist. The Church of Miracles and its Healing Well. My Formative Years at Carey Baptist College. Discipline and Corporal Punishment. Election to Presidency of the SCM. The End of WWII and an Outpouring of the Holy Spirit.

I WAS SENT TO ST. PAUL'S MILAGIRIYA SCHOOL WHERE I ATTENDED its Kindergarten. My father, being an Anglican Catechist, was well-known to many of the clergymen. I remember the day he took me to visit Rev. Paul Lucian Janz who was the vicar of the church. Any nervousness I felt walking into this elderly gentleman's office with my father was put at ease with Rev. Janz's ready smile.

Rev. Lucian Janz was a linguist who could read and speak seven languages. He opened the Bible to Psalm 23 and read it in Malayalam! Needless to say I was very much surprised and wondered at his ability to speak Malayalam which was a language not many people were familiar with.

The Church of St. Paul in Milagiriya, around which the school was built, was, back in the days of the Portuguese, a Roman Catholic church known as *Nossa Senhora dos Milagres* meaning 'our lady of Miracles'. '*Milagiriya*' is the 'sinhalised' name for the Portuguese word *milagres*, meaning 'miracles'[1].

There was a well, situated near the original church, and pilgrims

[1] *Ref:* "*St.Paul's Milagiriya*" - http://www.lankalibrary.com/phpBB/viewtopic.php?f=60&t=1334

from faraway places came to drink this water, which was reputed for its miraculous healing properties.

In 1955, I was confirmed in this church by the then Rt. Rev. Rollo Graham-Campbell the then Bishop of Colombo who, incidentally, was the last British Bishop of Colombo.

In 1947 I was enrolled as a student at Carey Baptist College starting at Grade 3. Carey College was the premier Baptist school in the island and was founded by Baptist Missionaries. Among them were Waldock and Spooner, the college Houses named after them. The college itself was named in honour of the English educator and Baptist missionary, William Carey, who founded the first Christian Missionaries in the East. The school is located at Kinsey Road in Borella, close to the Colombo Eye Hospital (or *As Wāttuwa* as the locals usually call it) and facing the Medical College. Opposite the college were the Roman Catholic Seminary and the Archbishop's House. During interval we could see young seminarians, all decked out in white coming out during their break.

The Principal of Carey College, Rev. W. M. P. Jayatunge was the school's first Ceylonese principal and the embodiment of a strict disciplinarian bordering on cruelty. He showed no mercy in exacting punishment on hapless students. He lived in a large, upstair bungalow overlooking the premises. When he walked the corridors of the college during class-hours, any student seeing him would run and hide, even if they were going to answer a call of nature. My classmates and I avoided him as best we could.

His classes were always on Order, Beauty and Discipline which were the watchwords he adhered to. Classes began at eight every morning and at 7:50 a recording of orchestra music would play, signalling all students to stand in line outside their classrooms. When the next record played we went into Assembly and took our seats. There, above the stage, in bold letters was inscribed "It is immoral to be satisfied with ugliness when beauty is within our reach".

A ruthless disciplinarian, mercy was not an attribute he possessed. I remember the day I walked out of my classroom after the sounding of the interval bell to find a group of boys staring at a student, stripped to his waist, glistening in sweat under a blazing sun. A humiliating punishment. And the crime? The young boy had not worn his school tie!

On another occasion, towards the end of a school day, the office boy – Roland was his name, as I recall – walked into class with a note for our Teacher. We were all to assemble in the Hall immediately. Such summons always meant someone was going to be caned in public.

The Principal stood on the platform, the staff behind him and over 700 students seated in front of him. He proclaimed the name of the student and said he had been caught smoking a cigarette. Furthermore, on searching his pockets a packet of cigarette was also found.

Cigarettes were very cheap in those days. The most expensive one was *Bristol*, next *3 Roses* and the cheapest among them was *Peacock*. He must have had one of the most expensive ones! The Principal first took a moment to instil on our young minds the dangers of smoking and how it could harm our lungs and our bodies. He then called the boy up onto the stage and asked him to stretch out his left hand. He drew out a long cane and in swift, merciless strokes, caned the boy three times. Next, he called for the boy's right hand and again, three bitter cuts.

While the boy stood there clutching his palms and rubbing them together in pain, the Principal asked him to go down the steps towards the main entrance of the school which faced Kinsey Road. Following the boy closely, they reached the front door. We had all turned around now to see what was going to happen. At the entrance, the Principal gave the boy such a hard kick that he nearly fell to the ground. The boy had received the ultimate punishment: Expulsion from school.

In those days, a student who was expelled could not seek to gain admission in any other school. There was just one institution that admitted such students: The Pembrook Academy – a school for dropouts and those who repeatedly failed their exams.

The fear that ran through the student body was great, a fear that was to grow when we realized that the Baptist Board would not take any action against such inhuman punishment. We cringed every time Roland came by with a chit calling for the students to assemble in the Hall.

It was reported much later that Principal Jayatunge was removed for reasons unknown and was succeeded by Rev. W. G. Wickremasinghe, a graduate of Kings College, London, and who held a Master's Degree.

The new principal was the complete opposite of his predecessor. Kind and friendly with a warm disposition, he was always dressed in a white suit. I was a boy of fifteen then and was so surprised when he began to teach us Christianity and English Literature. The only sort of principal I had known up till that point was one who represented fear and discipline and I could not believe that a principal of a school could be such a benevolent human being.

Each Friday the Christians had their service before going to classes. The Principal taught us choruses such as the 1914 verse by Charles A. Miles:

Wide, wide as the ocean, high as the Heaven above;
Deep, deep as the deepest sea is my saviour's love.
I, though so unworthy, still am a child of His care;
For His Word teaches me that His love reaches me everywhere.

Each week we sang these choruses at the Christian Assembly. I remember Stanley Jones the famous Methodist Missionary speak at the assembly. I do not recall the actual message but I can still recall the glow on his face and the white suit he wore. Stanley Jones was a close friend of Mahatma Ghandi and was held high in esteem by such men as Nehru and Patel, the freedom fighters of India.

Another speaker that I recall was Bakht Singh Chabra, also known as Brother Bakht Singh and the Apostle of India. A man who had founded over 600 churches, he had a voice so powerful, it reverberated throughout the halls. Years of open air ministry had tempered his voice to slice through the air like steel. It was no wonder he was called the Elijah of the 21st century.[2] He could quote over 1,200 Bible verses by heart and, like another Indian Christian missionary, Sadhu Sundar Singh, he was also converted from the Sikh faith. Dave Hunt, a Canadian Christian author and radio announcer once wrote of Brother Bakht Singh and his missionary work:

"The arrival of Bakht Singh turned the churches of Madras upside down... Crowds gathered in the open air, as many as 12,000 on one occasion to hear this man of God. Many seriously ill were healed when Bakht Singh prayed for them, even deaf and dumb began to hear and speak."

My own early efforts in Christian works saw me elected President of the Student Christian Movement (SCM) which was very popular in schools

[2] *Ref:* T. E. Koshy (March 1st 2008) *"Bakht Singh of India"*. Authentic Publishing.

at that time. The highlight was my being chosen to represent the Carey College at the Triennial Conference in Guntur India in 1957. As President, I was responsible for arranging the weekly programmes. I invited pastors from other denominations to come and address the Christian Assembly. Mr. Albrecht was the staff member who was in charge of the SCM. He was a Burgher gentleman who lived on our street down Swarna Road. Later, I was pleasantly surprised to meet him at Bethesda Hall for services.

My aim was to ensure that the Friday meetings were attractive and interesting, by inviting speakers to address our student body. I personally went with another student to invite the speakers, of course with the prior clearance of Mr. Albrecht.

Some of those who accepted our invitation was Rev. Roger Greenway of the Dutch Reformed Church (now the Christian Reformed Church of Sri Lanka) and Rev. Swinthin Fernando. I made it a point to involve as many students as possible in the programme. Planning these meetings would also include organising the music and whenever there was a need for a duet, I was always able call upon the Senapathiratne brothers who readily obliged. Needless to say, the experience I gained at the SCM was helpful in my later ministry.

With the end of the Second World War, while Europe was rebuilding itself and America was at peace, churches, especially in America, began to experience a fresh outpouring of the Holy Spirit.

4

The Pentecostal Revival. Post-war Healing Revivals Across the Globe. Billy Graham Preaches to Thousands. William Branham and Words of Wisdom and Knowledge. Oral Roberts' Healing Ministry. A.C. Valdez's Sri Lanka Crusade makes Front Page.

THE PENTECOSTAL REVIVAL FIRST BEGAN IN AZUSA STREET IN LOS Angeles California and is hailed as the origin of the Pentecostal movement[1]. Beginning with a meeting led by an African American preacher, William J. Seymour on April 14th, 1906, the outpouring of the Holy Spirit upon this rival of the Pentecostal Church was demonstrated in wide-spread speaking in tongues, personal spiritual experiences and, especially at that time, considered by the secular media to be unorthodox and even outrageous. However, it is that self same movement that historians consider to be the prime catalyst for a worldwide revival of the Christian Church.

Around 1947 and '48, the world witnessed a healing revival, the magnitude of which the Church had never before experienced since the Apostolic Era began. Billy Graham was preaching in a series of revival meetings in Los Angeles under circus tents erected at a parking lot. Since Billy Graham's ministry began in 1947, he had conducted over 400 crusades spanning 185 countries on six continents. It was Billy Graham who first coined the word 'crusades' after the medieval Christian forces that tried to conquer Jerusalem. His ardent preaching of the Gospel was

---

[1] *Ref:* Frank Bartleman *"Azusa Street"*. Bridge-Logos Publishers. ISBN 0-88270-439-7.

broadcast on radio and television, and according to some sources, more than 3.2 million people have responded to the invitation to accept Jesus Christ as their personal Saviour. Billy Graham formed an Evangelistic association and in all the crusades he conducted, took no "love offering", but was paid a regular salary from the Association. This brought credibility and accountability to evangelistic work.

William Branham came upon the scene and began to operate the gifts of the Spirit especially the Word of Wisdom and Word of Knowledge. An Angel of the Lord had appeared to him in his room, commissioning him to preach the gospel, with the promise that not even cancer would stand against his prayers. Branham was filling large stadiums both in the USA and abroad. He had the ability to call out from the podium the name, address, and the sickness a person was suffering from and instantly the person received healing.

It was at this same time Oral Roberts began his healing ministry in Oklahoma having been healed himself of tuberculosis. Roberts was a powerful preacher and his tent crusades drew thousands across America. Roberts was also the pioneer of TV evangelism with his program '*The Abundant Life*' reaching 80% of Americans by 1957. At his faith healing crusades, thousands upon thousands of sick people would stand in line so that he could pray for them. In his ministry, he conducted over 300 crusades across the globe and had personally laid hands on more than two million people.

The astounding reports of these men were in publications that reached us here in Sri Lanka. With amazement, I read and saw the pictures of young Billy Graham preaching and calling people to come to the altar for salvation. This was in the *Decision Magazine. The Abundant Life* magazine showed pictures of Oral Roberts praying for the sick and large crowds attending his crusades. For the first time, we were witnessing a preaching of the Gospel to huge crowds, under these tents, that looked so different to regular church services.

It was also during this period, amidst the Healing Revivals held in America and England that a man called A. C. Valdez came to Sri Lanka under the auspices of the Assemblies of God. This was over February and March of 1954. A tent was erected at Shrubbery Gardens and Valdez was drawing quite a crowd. The news spread far and wide that Valdez had the gift of healing and people from all walks of life came each evening to hear him preach. At the conclusion of his sermon, he would sit on a chair (in the manner of Oral Roberts) and pray individually for each sick person. I too went for prayer and he took my hand into his big huge white hands and prayed for my healing.

The *Daily News* ran a story of his tent meeting on the front page resulting in an ever-increasing the attendance. This was probably the first national newspaper ever to endorse a Christian Healing Crusade.

Even the Minister of Health, if I remember correctly, had asked him to come and pray for the sick in the hospitals. Valdez agreed to pray as long as he was also allowed to first preach to the sick beforehand. I believe that this must have been politely turned down.

5

The Approaching Sounds of the Horsemen of the Apocalypse. Independence and Sinhala Nationalism. The 'Sinhala Only' Act. The Rise of the Red Horseman. The B-C Pact and the Road to Communal Riots of 1958. The Assassination of a Prime Minister. The Redemption of Vimala Wijewardena. Undercurrents of Anti-Christianity.

Soon after independence, the spirit of nationalism began to agitate for reforms in all sectors of society. The Sinhalese felt that they had been discriminated by their former Colonial rulers and demanded priority be given both to the Sinhala language and Buddhism. English was the language of commerce and trade. The public service and mercantile sectors consisted of large numbers of Tamil-speaking people. The grievances of the Sinhala majority were that large portions of the hill-country were being gobbled up by the descendants of the Indian labour force, brought to the country by the British, to work in tea estates.

Banks, Mercantile firms, Municipalities, *Katchcheries*[1], Ports and Customs employed, in their view, too many Tamils. Universities had a disproportionate number of Tamils and the Sinhala youth felt marginalized. For a Sinhalese to send a telegram it had to be first translated into English. Colombo had a substantial population of Tamils who owned houses and lands and this made the Sinhala people feel deprived of their rights.

The medium of education was in English right up to University and this was a barrier for the Sinhala educated to have a University Education.

[1] Government regulatory offices

English was the favoured language of their Colonial Masters. For five hundred years, the Portuguese, the Dutch and the English established schools and the beginning of conversion to Christianity was through these schools and orphanages. There was a widespread feeling that Catholic nuns working in hospitals were also indirectly influencing Buddhists. All this had to change. The General Election of 1956 paved the way for these reforms.

In the General Election of 1956, the Sri Lanka Freedom Party (SLFP), led by S. W. R. D. Bandaranaike, won a landslide victory against the United National Party (UNP). The SLFP, along with the *Mahajana Eksath Peremuna* or the People's United Front, held 90 seats in parliament, whilst the UNP were reduced to just 9 seats. Bandaranaike promised to introduce Sinhala as the only official language of the country, within 24 hours. A few others parties such as the socialist Lanka *Sama Samaja* Party (LSSP) and the communist party opposed this 'Sinhala Only Bill', but later accepted the language policy.

Dr. Colvin R. Silva, a prominent lawyer was known to have stated:

> *"Do we want a single nation or do we want two nations? Do we want a single state or do we want two? Do we want one Ceylon or do we want two? And above all, do we want an independent Ceylon which must necessarily be united and single Ceylon, or two bleeding halves of Ceylon which can be gobbled up by every ravaging imperialist monster that may happen to range the Indian Ocean? These are issues that in fact we have been discussing under the form and appearance of language issue."*

The policies of the new Government left the Tamils feeling marginalized. And even the partial reversal of Sinhala Only Bill – the so-called 'Sinhala Only, Tamil Also' compromise – did little to alleviate rising tension.

Tamils in general felt that new jobs would go to those proficient in Sinhala and not in English. The Burgher community began to migrate to Australia *en masse*, fearing that they too would be victimized. Tamils began to return to India and others to Europe and Canada in search of new pastures. When the Sinhala Only Act was debated in Parliament, some Federal Party Members of Parliament squatted before the Parliament building in a fasting protest, demanding that they be heard and the legislation be amended or withdrawn. While they were seated along the walls of the Parliament building, several men came and forcibly dragged them away and cast them into the sea, which was right in front of the Parliament. Evidently, the Police was unable to prevent force being used against the elected Tamil representatives.

The Bill had had its intended effect. Whilst in the mid-1950s the civil service had been largely Tamil, by 1970, it was almost entirely Sinhalese, with thousands of Tamils forced to resign due to lack of fluency in Sinhala. And so the distant thunder of the hooves of the Four Horsemen of the Apocalypse was heard over the land. The cry for a separate Tamil state had begun to take shape. Pandora's Box was opened and the country would never be the same again.

The SLFP mandate was to make Sinhala the official language *per se*. The party received this mandate at a democratic election held in 1956. Now the Government had only to bring in new legislation and rules to ensure that this new policy was followed by all.

One immediate change that came into play was vehicle license plates. Earlier registration numbers began with the letters in the name Ceylon (*i.e.* CEY was the last of the English letters that was used on the license plate.) S. W. R. D. Bandaranaike's Cadillac was the now on the road bearing the famous – or infamous – '1 ශ්‍රී' (Sri) License plate. The policy was now imposed all across the island, including Jaffna and other northern towns where most of the Tamils lived.

In 1958, I was a student at Aquinas University College in Borella. This institution was the brain child of Fr. Peter Pillai who was the former Rector of St. Joseph's College, Colombo. Here I was preparing for the London Advanced Level examination. It was a two-year course and the final examination was conducted by London examiners. The Rector of this college was Fr. Balasuriya from the Oblates of Mary Immaculate Order (OMI). Fr. Kuriacose, a friend of my father, taught British History, and Mr. Srinivasam, an Indian from Tamil Nadu who quoted profusely from memory.

The students and staff at Aquinas were from all nationalities. There were Sinhalese, Tamil, Muslims and Burghers. Regardless of their religious background, there were no racial prejudices evident. We were members of one large family and helped each other whenever possible. Since we lived in Havelock town, I usually got a ride home from either Munasinghe or Keegal who lived close by.

The events of 1957 and 1958 were harbingers of the riots, war and the bloodshed that lasted thirty long years, almost as long as the 30-year North European war in 1618-48. The Red Horseman was upon us, bringing bloodshed and destruction.

During this period, between 1957 and 1958, there emerged a silent opposition to Christian conversion and church expansion. For many years *Radio Ceylon* was broadcasting programmes by Billy Graham and Oral Roberts. *Radio Ceylon* was paid by the Americans for their air time. Along with the Sinhala Only Bill, there was an undercurrent that was anti-Christian. The Government abruptly stopped these programmes, leaving only the *Back to the Bible* program, which was also eventually taken off the air, end-1958. I vividly remember listening to the last *Back to the Bible* Gospel programme on our white Murphy Radio. Anti-Christian winds were now beginning to blow across the island.

* * *

The background to the Bandaranaike-Chelvanayakam (B-C) Pact was the forerunner of the deadly riots of 1958. With the passing of the Sinhala Only Bill in 1957, the Tamils, who formed a substantial portion of the population, felt that their culture, language and position were now under threat. To appease the unease of the Tamils, Bandaranaike entered into negotiations with the Federal Party and drew up an accord to be presented to Parliament to guarantee the reasonable use of Tamil in the north and East. This was opposed by a large section of people. In April 1957, the bill was ready to be presented to the Parliament when, on the 9th of that month, 100 monks and a mob of 300 other people came to the Prime Minister's residence at Rosemead Place demanding that the Pact be abrogated. The PM talked to them and tried to convince them that it should be accepted. They refused and demanded that he immediately cancel it. The PM walked into his house, came out with the copy and tore it in front of the mob. He was also coerced into making a statement in writing that the Bill would be ditched.[2]

---

[2] Patrick Peebles (2006-08-30). "*The History of Sri Lanka*". Greenwood Press. ISBN 978-0-313-33205-0.

The monks and the mob left. The Bill was torn to pieces. No one can deny the symbolism of that one act. From that moment on, the tearing apart of the nation began. It would take decades of war and bloodshed before unity and harmony were restored. The Pearl of the Indian Ocean now became the tear drop of the Indian Ocean. From that point onwards, the country would bleed not only from the head, but from the feet as well – both in the north and in the south.

I remember passing Rosmead Place that eventful day. I used to cycle along the road on my way back from School. On that particular day, as I approached the house of the PM, I saw the huge crowd of people gathered outside his residence, shouting slogans and waving their hands in the air. There were very few policemen guarding the house since no one expected people to come and make such a demand (it is good to remember that such was the peace up until that time that when the PM went to see a film at the Regal Theatre in Fort, he was accompanied by just one constable). When I saw the commotion, I decided to take another route back home.

On the 22nd of May I left college earlier than usual with news of Tamils being attacked and Tamil shops being set ablaze in many parts of Colombo. I rushed home as quickly as I could to find the neighbourhood buzzing with the news that riots had broken out across the nation. This was the first island-wide riot and the Tamils were the target. It lasted for five days. Almost all of the victims were Tamils. Tamil houses were attacked, shops were burnt, and in some, Tamils were burnt alive. The train going to Batticaloa was also attacked and Tamils were pulled out and assaulted.

In response to these actions, the Tamils attacked Sinhalese farmers and looted and emptied shops. When the smoke and fire had died down, around 300 people had been killed on both sides. Over 12,000 Tamils took refuge in schools. Royal College was full of Tamils scared to stay at, or return home. The Government engaged five European ships to transport them to Jaffna. The tragedy was that most of them had never been to Jaffna and were forced to return back to their homes in Colombo. The Red Horsemen of the Apocalypse now was riding into the heart of this Island. The soil was soaked with the blood of both the Sinhalese and Tamils.

The Army was called out and they patrolled the streets at night. During the day, soldiers were stationed at all the major junctions to prevent any looting and violence.

When the rioting was brought under control through emergency rule and the martial law, the schools were reopened. I rode a bus from the Spinning and Weaving Mills and got down at The Eye Hospital junction. I looked towards Lipton Circus, where six roads merged and saw the roundabout beset with soldiers. On seeing them I was hit with a strong thought: "Never again will this land have any peace!" How true this thought was! We lived through a thirty-year bloody war and a rule by emergency that covered most of our lives. The Red Horseman had carried out his damning purpose on the island.

* * *

S. W. R. D. Bandaranaike was born to a wealthy family and was baptized an Anglican Christian. He later, converted to Buddhism. He was the fourth prime minister of Sri Lanka and was assassinated on the 26th of September 1959 in his home. A delegation came to see the PM and when they said that a monk had arrived, the PM stood up and bowed his head with palms pressed together in reverence and respect. The monk, Talduwe Somarama Thero pulled out a pistol from beneath his robes and shot the PM point blank. The Prime Minister was rushed to hospital where he died the next day. The monk was assaulted and later also taken to hospital. There was utter pandemonium in all quarters when the news reached the people. The PM had only served three years and was sixty years old when he was killed; assassinated before his term of office ended.

The subsequent trial sentenced Somarama Thero, 45, to death. But the trial had also proven that Somarama had only been the triggerman. The instigator and chief plotter had been Mapitigama Buddharakkitha Thero, the 41-year-old high priest of the Kelaniya temple – a temple that the Buddhists believe a visit to can cleanse one of one's sins entirely. It was this self-same temple that had visited when he had won the election, and, in token of his gratitude, taken his entire cabinet to, for the customary post-inaugural rites. He also gave the post of Minister of Health to Buddharakkitha's friend, the widow Vimala Wijewardene, then aged 47.

It was widely believed that Buddharakkitha Thero was uneasy with the policies of the PM and feared that both the race and religion of the Sinhala people were in peril. Several people, including Vimala Wijewardene, had been frequent visitors to the temple and Buddharakkitha also spent time in Wijewardene's house. Somarama, according to reports was an unwilling assassin and is known to have stated during his trial: "I have done this thing to a man who did me no wrong – for the sake of my religion, my language and my race." This statement he later disavowed.

Buddharakkitha, Wijewardene and several others were arrested and tried in courts. Somarama was accused of murder and condemned to death by hanging. According to the *Time* magazine of July 13, 1962, prison officials reported that, on the eve of his execution, Somarama had himself baptized as a Christian.[3]

Vimala Wijewardene was arrested and imprisoned, accused of conspiring to murder the Prime Minister. During her incarceration she was visited by two sisters from the Pentecostal Mission who gave her a Bible and prayed for her on several occasions. Once, when Vimala's daughter came to visit her in prison, she was quite worried that her mother seemed to be quite at peace with herself. When she asked her mother why the change in countenance, she replied that she had started to read the Bible and pray. At the end of the trial, she was released, while Somarama was hanged and Buddharakkitha was sentenced to life imprisonment.

Wijewardene was once such a staunch Buddhist that she had even gone to Kataragama, a pilgrimage town sacred to Buddhists, Hindus and the indigenous Vedda people of Sri Lanka, where she performed the '*kavadi*', an ecstatic dance ritual emphasizing debt bondage. The dance is named after the *kavadi*, which is a heavy wooden structure, carried on the shoulder of the dancers. Made of two semicircular pieces of wood which are bent and attached to a cross structure that can be balanced on the shoulder of the dancer, the *kavadi* is often decorated with flowers or peacock feathers and some can weigh up to 30 kilos.

Several years later, we conducted an evangelistic meeting at Saraswathy Hall organized by brother, M. C. Mathew and Hugh Kanagasabay. At the end of the meeting, I was introduced to Wijewardene. I had the privilege of laying my hands upon her head to receive the Baptism of the Holy Spirit. I was overjoyed to see her happy face and her kind demeanour.

Several years later, Mr. Felix Dias Bandaranaike, the nephew of S. W. R.

[3] *Ref:* http://www.time.com/time/magazine/article/0,9171,827402,00.html

D. Bandaranaike, visited us in Kandy and spent several hours with us. At the end we prayed for him too, with laying on of hands, so that he would receive the Holy Spirit.

* * *

Most schools and colleges across the island were established by the Portuguese, the Dutch and the British. Among them was S. Thomas College in Mount Lavinia near the sea, where D. S. Senanayake, the first Prime Minister, and S. W. R. D. Bandaranaike, the fourth Prime Minister, were students. Royal College was at the heart of Colombo and former Prime Minister Ranil Wickremasinghe was a student of this school. The premier Catholic schools were St. Peter's College and St. Joseph's College in Darley Road. St. Bridget's Convent, the girl's school, was in Cinnamon Gardens and both Sirimavo and Chandrika Bandaranaike were students of this school. In every city there were Christian schools managed by the different denominations. There were a large number of schools established by the American Missionaries that produced outstanding doctors and civil servants. There were also a number of Buddhist and Hindu schools managed by their respective organizations. These schools catered to millions of students.

When Mrs. Bandaranaike came to power, she embarked on a massive nationalization process. Some bus companies, financially supported by the opposing United National Party, were nationalised and so was the Colombo harbour.

In 1961, Mrs. Bandaranaike nationalized 2,500 private schools across the island. The schools in Jaffna, which were mostly Christian and Hindu, were most affected. They were privately managed but financially funded by the Government. Sri Lanka provided free health and medical treatment to all its citizens and free education from Kindergarten to University.

Patrick Peebles, in his book *The History of Sri Lanka,* says that the schools in Jaffna were most affected as these newly nationalized schools had now to teach students in the "mother tongue" – not in the language spoken at home but according to the "race or ethnicity of the child". The Tamil student now could not study in Sinhala or English but had to be enrolled in the Tamil Medium. The Sinhala students, even though the language spoken at home was English, could not study in English but in Sinhala. This was the island-wide policy instigated by the National Education Council.

A child joins a school when he or she is 4 or 5 years old. After twelve years, the Tamil student comes out and discovers that he cannot get a job in the Public or Government departments as Sinhala is must for new entrants. The Sinhala student leaves school and looks out for employment but finds it nigh on impossible to get a job as the mercantile sectors, such as Banking, Shipping and Teaching, were looking for candidates with a good knowledge of English. Thousands of Sinhala students, after 10-12 years of school, found that companies prefer people with a good knowledge of spoken and written English. The year was 1970 – most Sinhala students who had just completed their education were between the years of 16 and 18. Their hopes were shattered. Their parents were anxiously waiting for them to get a decent job and earn a living.

In my opinion, I firmly believe that the alienation, and depriving the Sinhala youth the opportunity to study in the medium they desired, in turn, resulted in their inability to find employment and led to the infamous and bloody revolt and Che Guevara Revolution of 1971.

In the beginning of the sixties, under Mrs. Bandaranaike, going overseas in search of jobs in Europe or Canada was almost impossible. A person could not purchase a ticket if someone paid for it abroad in foreign currency. A person may have all the money to travel but was forbidden to buy the ticket in rupees. The stringent exchange control laws were similar to the Socialistic countries of the world. Young people were trapped in the island. The Government had held a monopoly in every sector.

In 1970, the United National Party, which was ruling for a few years, was soundly defeated and the SLFP led by Mrs. Bandaranaike, had come to power again with the help of the communist and some other parties.

6

Fr. Balasuriya and Liberation Theology. I Become a Banker. Bethesda Hall and the Beginning of the Charismatic Movement. The Tale of Two Funerals.

I LEFT AQUINAS AFTER SITTING FOR THE LONDON ADVANCED LEVEL Examination. Before leaving, I went to meet Fr. Tissa Balasuriya who was the Registrar/Warden of the college. Fr. Balasuriya belonged to the OMI Order. He was an active proponent of Liberation Theology, a political movement in the Catholic Church that interpreted the teachings of Christ to show that the church must oppose all types of injustices whether social, economical or political. This movement was especially active in South America.

In 1990, Fr. Balasuriya published a book called *"Mary and Human Liberation"*[1] and the Roman Catholic Church concluding it was bordering on heresy, defrocked him although they later lifted his excommunication and re-instated him.

He was a friendly and caring person who took genuine interest in the welfare of the poor. In the afternoon of that day I went to his office and thanked him for what Aquinas had done and for how much it had meant to me. I was emboldened enough to ask him, "Father, do not misunderstand, but may I ask you a question?"

He looked at me and said, "Young man, go ahead."

"Do you have the assurance of salvation?" I asked. A bold question to

[1] *Ref:* Tissa Balasuriya (1997) *"Mary and Human Liberation"*. ISBN 978-1563382253

ask a man of Fr. Balasuriya's stature, to be sure!

He looked slightly flustered and then asked of me, "Where in the Bible does it say you can be saved?" He probably did not expect me to be able to reply.

"In the Book of Acts, chapter 16 and verse 12 where it says: 'Believe on the Lord Jesus Christ, and you will be saved, you and your household.'"

Fr. Balasuriya was visibly taken aback. "Oh! You seem to have studied the Bible well!" he said, and, rising to our feet, we shook hands and he said to me, "I wish you God's blessings."

While I am penning these very words it was announced that Fr. Balasuriya had passed away and the burial would take place at the Borella *Kanatte*[2] on the 19th of January, 2013.

Not long after my meeting with Fr. Balasuriya, at the end of 1959, I was applying to various companies for employment. Deep down, I wanted to join the ranks of the Central Bank of Ceylon as it promised a good salary and other perks. I prayed and felt that I would receive what I had asked for in prayer. I went for in for an interview and was overjoyed to be asked to report in for duty on the 20th of January 1960.

* * *

Bethesda Gospel Hall was started by a group of Businessmen from England who were working in Sri Lanka. They met in a rented house for worship and, among them, was an Anglican Chinese lady. Her name was Amelia Loos. Her husband was a well-to-do attorney and she offered to help build a hall for services. She purchased the land and built the hall and furnished it. It was dedicated to God on the 3rd of April, 1919.

I lived down Swarna Road, where, at the end of the 1950s, there was a building boom with forty to fifty new houses built and rented out, and a number of Burgher families moved in.

The street led to the bank of the old Dutch canal, which was our playground. One evening the youth fellowship of Bethesda Gospel Hall, came to our street and showed a film produced by the Moody Bible Institute. After the film, several young people testified and I was

---

[2] *Kannatte* means Cemetery

impressed by their joy and friendliness. They talked to me and invited me to their youth meetings which were held on a Tuesday. The Church had a separate hall where we played table tennis, and a lawn for badminton. After sweating it out through the film and subsequent meeting, we were offered a helping of Orange Barley which we gladly gulped down. There were about twenty youth who then sang choruses and someone gave a message from the Bible. I always looked forward to the Tuesday youth meetings and rushing home afterwards would turn on the radio to the Commercial Service to listen to the *"Hit Parade"* which featured songs sung by artistes like Pat Boone, Gene Autry, and The Platters.

There was no television in Sri Lanka at this time and there were only four channels on *Radio Ceylon*. The Commercial Service, the English service, and the Tamil and Sinhala service. You could not buy airtime for a Christian programme on any of the local stations regardless of how much you were willing to pay. The perception was that if Christian radio messages were heard, Buddhists and Hindus would be converted to Christianity. However on the Commercial Service we were able to buy time and broadcast the Gospel to India. Those in Sri Lanka could tune-in if they used the shortwave station, which, though not easy to tune into, was not impossible to hear. Apparently, the Sri Lankan government had absolutely no qualms about the Indians getting converted by listening to the messages broadcast on the Commercial Service of Ceylon! They gladly sold air time to Christians! However since the FEBC (Far East Broadcasting Corporation), an international Christian Missions organisation which broadcast the gospel on radio was heard in Sri Lanka on shortwave, few took advantage of the offer.

I began attending the youth meetings at Bethesda Gospel Hall and then the evening Sunday's services and special meetings sponsored by the church. On Sunday mornings I attended the Good Shepherd Anglican Church at Jawatte Road in Thimbirigasyaya as did the rest of my family. My father was the Catechist/Pastor of the church along with Rev. C. C. I. Abraham.

Dr. Sam Kamalason from Madras used to visit Bethesda and preach powerful sermons. He had a marvellous baritone voice which was heard all the way to Dickmans Road. The old songs were reborn after Kamalason sang them!

Gradually I began to attend the evening service and also the mid-week prayer meeting at Bethesda. The Wednesday prayer service, I first began attending, had about twelve people. The Elders faithfully attended the service. There was Fred Collette, a very friendly man who was worked at the Colombo Municipal Council before he migrated to Australia. Brother Classen, who always prayed fervently on Wednesdays, was another charming brother. Lewis, Janz and Hobbs from England were also amongst the elders. The brethren did not permit women to pray in public but they were allowed to pray in a private room. Most of the members of Bethesda were expatriates from Britain, a number of Burghers and a sprinkling of locals.

Shortly after I began attending, Fred Collette's wife passed away and the funeral was held at *Kanatte*. I attended the funeral and heard then sing and then Mr. Classen stood before the assembled congregation and began to speak. I remember in the background the sun was setting. Classen always wore a suit and tie. His voice was powerful and he spoke about the future hope believers have in Christ. There was no wailing and weeping but a solemn and sombre atmosphere prevailed. This was the first Christian funeral that I had ever attended. I rode my bicycle, home, deep in thought. Here was a group of people who believed with absolute certainty, of a hope of reunion with their loved ones, even after death.

We lived at No. 74 Swarna Road and our immediate neighbour lived at No. 76. There was no wall or fence to separate our houses. The father of the family was ill for a long while and one evening a group of people came by, chanting and beating a drum in the garden. Evidently these were a type of witch doctors or *Katadiyas* who claimed to cure the sick by exorcism. Before they could take a step forward in 'curing' their patient, they had to first locate the buried charm or talisman that the enemy had buried.

After several hours of more chanting and beating of drums, some men started digging and they unearthed a bronze amulet which they showed to the other members of the family. The chanting recommenced. This was the first excavation of a charm that I witnessed. There was a heavy spirit of oppression and fear that engulfed the area, more so for us, their next door neighbours!

Not long after, the father died, and for three days there was uncontrollable weeping and wailing. The wife, as soon as he drew his last breath, began to beat upon her breast and wail with all her daughters joining in. My mother went inside the house and tried to persuade the wife to stop beating her breasts but that did not work. Even today, this practiced is carried on, especially in India and Pakistan. On the day of the funeral, the eldest son collapsed as they were about to close the coffin, stricken with grief.

The Christian funeral and the death of our neighbour took place within a short time of each other. I had witnessed a funeral where the family were beating themselves and collapsing with grief and another where the husband and relatives stood bravely as the casket was lowered into the earth. The two funerals made a lasting impression on me; one full of despair and the other full of hope through Jesus Christ.

7

The Open and Exclusive Brethren Assembly. Don Rubesh, Bruce Ker and Jim Cook. The Swami and the Sunset. My Baptism of the Holy Spirit. The Evangelical Tract Club. Origin and Growth of Pentecostalism and The Charismatics.

IT WAS THE YEAR 1960. I WAS NOW ACTIVELY INVOLVED AT THE Bethesda Gospel Hall. An Open Brethren Assembly, Bethesda was also called the Plymouth Brethren and these evangelical Christian assemblies rose up in England in the 1820's. Open Brethren Assemblies are different to Exclusive Brethren Assemblies even though they share the same roots. Each Assembly acts independently, although there is much communication between them.

The beginning of the split, which formed the Open and Exclusive Assemblies, took place in 1845 when Wills Newton, the elder of the largest Brethren Assembly was denounced by John Nelson Darby on the issue of Prophecy and Organization. George Ferdinand Müller is one of the most famous Brethren leaders who lived in Bristol and was director of the Ashley Down Orphanage.

There are many stories of Gods miraculous provision through the prayer of these Brethren. In 1959, there were more than 600 assemblies in the USA and 300 in Canada. Bethesda recognized the office of the Elder and Deacon and had no fulltime Pastor or Evangelist. There was no membership roll or offerings taken in public.

T. M. Jayawardena was the Principal of the Training College in

Maharagama. He was a teacher of the Bible who taught the Word with clarity and profound insight. I will never forget his teaching on the Tabernacle, where every material in the Tabernacle, according to him, spoke of Christ. He displayed a miniature Tabernacle and all of us young people never forgot these lessons.

He edited a magazine called the *"Advent Courier"* which contained interesting Bible studies. He travelled often to Australia and New Zealand. When his former Assembly refused to recommend him to the Assemblies in New Zealand he joined the Bethesda Assembly. The reason for his leaving his earlier assembly and joining us was not fully known. One thing is certain: we must endeavour to keep the unity of the Spirit until we all come to the unity of faith. Spiritual unity is vital for the sustenance of faith and knowledge in the Body of Christ. Those who claim to be doctors of the "Law and Testimony" may later be found wanting in affection and love for the Brethren and be flawed in their walk with God.

Don Rubesh came to Sri Lanka in 1956 and established the *Back to the Bible* broadcast office and aired programs on *Radio Ceylon*. Rubesh was a tall, well-built American who gave the evangelical ministry a shot in the arm through his radio ministry and personal involvement, by successfully uniting the evangelical-minded people from different denominations. He had a large family and they lived in Skelton Avenue off Dickman's Road.

Since Bethesda was an Open Brethren church and accepted Evangelicals, Rubesh used to preach regularly at the evening service. Rubesh belonged to the Evangelical Alliance Mission but was loaned to the *Back to the Bible* Broadcast mission because of his interest in spreading the Gospel through Radio and promoted evangelism in country. He was a musician and used to play the accordion and the Vibro Harp at the evening services, although the Brethren were not too excited about music other than the piano.

The singing at the church was now enhanced by these musical instruments. Miss Toussaint was a very modest sister whose fingers seemed to dance across the keys of the piano whenever she played it. The evening services soon saw many visitors flocking to enjoy the vibrant music and preaching.

Rubesh was a pioneer in the formation of the present Evangelical Fellowship which is now known as the Evangelical Alliance of Sri Lanka. His son Ted Rubesh later married Renate. Hildegard's brother Werner used to hold Bible Studies in his home in Aalen, Germany. We visited him and first met Renate at his house.

In 1984, on our way to Sri Lanka from California, we met Renate again in Germany. When we prayed for her, something had quickened in her spirit like never before. Right after prayer, she said she felt like a new person and told Werner she must come to Sri Lanka with us. Renate and Hildegard's niece, Heidi, stayed with us at our home in Kandy for some time. One day, Ted and Renate went on a hike to Hantana. They have been hiking together ever since.

Bruce Ker was the son of a Baptist Missionary who worked in northern India. He and his wife Esther came to Sri Lanka from the Philippines, sent by the Conservative Baptist Foreign Mission Society in Oregon. Since the local Baptist churches were leaning towards liberalism, they may have found the Denominational structure too binding.

Bethesda Hall was now coming to be known as the home of Evangelicals who were promoting the Gospel through radio, literature, preaching, youth rallies and camps. Bruce Ker was a graduate of the Dallas Theological Seminary and a genial personality. He was a tall, lanky person and reminded me of the actor James Stuart of Hollywood fame. Ker was one of the friendliest and most loving people one could ever meet. His preaching was expository and user-friendly. Young people rallied around him and saw in him a mentor and a person to emulate. Now there were a number of youth attending the services. Among them were Edema, Sam Sherrad, Ranjit De Silva and Maurice Herft. We used to gather in his house at Fredrika Road and have Bible studies each week.

We will never forget when, after an evening of Bible study, Ker took us out into the lawn and told us to look up at the sky. We gazed up at the black, star-speckled night sky and saw, to our astonishment, the Soviet satellite Sputnik, the first earth Satellite, moving across the heavens like a miniscule light bulb! It was launched on October 1957 and burned up in the atmosphere on 4th January 1958. The space age had begun and so did the Space Race. Today we use wireless phones and GPS systems without a thought to those who made it possible. Was this a fulfilment of the prophecy which says that in the last days "knowledge shall increase and men shall run to and fro"? *(Daniel 12:4)*

During this time, several young men came for prayer and felt a burden to win souls. Among those who demonstrated a burning desire for saving souls was Tissa Weerasinghe, a young man of 17 years with a brilliant mind and a student of S. Thomas' College, Mt. Lavinia. Tissa was an able communicator and we went on to hold several campaigns in up-country Sri Lanka. His scholarly ability won him many awards at Fuller Seminary and he holds a Ph.D. Today he is the senior pastor of one of the largest Churches in Sri Lanka – The Calvary Church, Kirulapone. Colombo.

Ranjit De Silva was one of our loyal prayer warriors on the team. He resigned from his job at Carson Cumberbatch and went to Bible College in Dehra Dun, India. Then to Multnomah Bible College and finally obtained his Ph.D from Fuller Theological Seminary in Pasadena, California. He served as the Principal of the Lanka Bible College from 1980 to 1988. Ranjit had an uncanny ability to locate potential leaders who he placed in responsible positions.

Sam Rajendran was a very jovial and humorous brother who knew when to crack a joke just at the right moment to diffuse tensions. He was deeply spiritual and went with us on many campaigns. He married Esther and migrated to Australia. We have deeply missed him in Sri Lanka

Sam Sherrad became the Director of Youth for Christ in Sri Lanka and then president of the World Youth for Christ, a position once held by Billy Graham in 1948. He worked at the Government Press and resigned to join the ministry.

Preman Serasinghe was another student from the same school who began his ministry within the tea estates, conducted healing meetings and boldly preached that Christ is the Healer and many were saved and healed.

Jim Cook was invited by Bruce Ker to come to Sri Lanka. He had an athletic figure and was fond of flexing his muscles. He and his wife,

Shirley and their two children became part of the Bethesda family. Jim Cook was a powerful speaker who preached regularly at evening services. With these three American missionary preachers and their infectious passion for souls, the congregation at Bethesda began to grow. The music was outstanding, the preaching was dynamic and the fellowship was contagious. More and more people found the Lord and the news of the meetings began to spread around Colombo. The entire De Silva family from the Narahenpita Flats found the Lord as their Saviour and became regular attendees.

I remember being seated next to Ranjit De Silva when he raised his hand for salvation, responding to Bruce Ker's invitation. I was surprised to see him read the Scripture at the next youth meeting so fervently. Jim Cook was a star basketball player who played for his state in America. He quickly formed a Bethesda Youth Basketball Club and began playing with other schools. His coaching was noticed by the Sri Lanka Basketball Association who invited him to coach the Sri Lankan team that toured Pakistan. Needless to say, we were now very proud of our coach and our own players.

We were totally consumed with the desire to win souls and began to distribute stacks of literature on the streets and buses. Our aim was to locate a spot where the maximum number of people gathered and hand these tracts to them as quickly as possible. Our target was hospital gates before they opened. Hundreds of people would be waiting to see their loved ones in hospital and as such were very receptive. Then we went to schools after classes were over. As the boys came streaming out at the sound of the dismissal bell, we would stand near the gate with bundles of tracts and within a short time they would all be gone. We did this at Royal College and Wesley College and even gave an altar call while distribution was going on. No one stopped us, although they probably admired our youthful enthusiasm.

One evening, at around six o'clock, we were getting ready to distribute tracts at the Wellawatte Railway station just in time for the trains to come from Colombo loaded with passengers, many of whom got off at that station. The train arrived and scores of people began to pour out of the compartments. We wanted to reach the most number of people in the shortest of time.

The train departed and a few were still on the platform and amongst them was a Hindu *Saniyasini* or "Holy Man". He was about sixty years old and was clad in the yellow robe worn by a Sadu. He had long matted hair and a *tilak* or spot of holy ash on his forehead. Some believe the ash is a reminder that one day you will turn back into dust and ashes. He carried a small bag on his shoulder and we gave him a tract. He scanned it and then looked at us for a moment before proclaiming, "for me, God is everywhere and everything. Look!" he said "at that sun. That is my God."

At that very moment the setting sun disappeared over the horizon. Sam called out, "O swami, where is your god? Has he disappeared?"

Not to be undone and in the fading twilight he looked up and saw a dim 40 watt bulb hanging from the platform roof. He said, "Look! That light is my god!"

That very moment, we heard a soft but distinct *'POP'* as the light bulb blew its filament. We were all taken aback and even Sam was speechless, but not for long. "O swami, where is your god now?" he called out and you could hear the triumph in his voice.

The Swami had a look of bewilderment on his face and slowly walked away, shaking his head with tract in hand. Several bystanders, who were watching with interest at what had unfolded, stepped forward and accepted our tracts. Needless to say we had a very responsive audience.

* * *

We formed the Evangelical Tract Club (ETC) to distribute Christian Literature to the masses who were mostly Buddhist, Hindus and Moslems. One small paper advert in the classified column of the *Sunday Observer*, offering a free Gospel of John, brought in over 150 letters to No. 21, Dickman's Road, Colombo 4. How thrilled we were to slip those Gospel portions inside the brown envelopes and post those copies to people who asked for them. One day, while we were preparing to send those stacks of letters, Bruce Ker walked in unannounced and gave us three sheets of stamps to be affixed to the envelopes. The responses continued and later the ETC evolved into the 'River of Life' Correspondence Course with its office in Kandy.

8

The Origin and Growth of the Pentecostal Movement. Pentecostalism in Sri Lanka. The Charismatic Renewal. USA, Canada and the Jesus Movement. Charismata in Bethesda and its Impact. The Price for Renewal.

IT WOULD BE APPROPRIATE TO BRIEFLY DISCUSS THE ORIGIN AND growth of the Pentecostal movement before talking about the Charismatic Renewal. As mentioned earlier on, Pentecostalism began in April, 1906, when a group of people praying in Azusa Street, California, were filled with the Holy Spirit and spoke in tongues.[1] Classical Pentecostalism was a revival movement with the Church that emphasized a direct experience with God in receiving the Baptism of the Holy Spirit and speaking in tongues. They believed that the Pentecostal experience is the last outpouring of the Spirit before the return of Jesus Christ. They said what we are experiencing is a reflection of the Apostolic Age which was attended by signs and wonders. This movement was also called Full Gospel.

The largest Pentecostal church in the world, located in Seoul Korea, is called the Central Full Gospel Church with a membership of one million people. The Pentecostal Movement spread like wildfire to Europe, Scandinavia, India and to many other parts of the world.

The Pentecostal Movement began in Sri Lanka with the visit of Anna

[1] *Ref:* Frank Bartleman (1980) *"Azusa Street"*. Bridge-Logos Publishers. ISBN 0-88270-439-7.

Lewini, a Danish actress, in 1922[2]. Through her ministry, many young Sri Lankan Christians received the Baptism of the Holy Spirit. Some of their sons and daughters are alive today and are leaders in the church. My father spoke glowingly of Anna Lewini and the impact she had on those number of Christians who were strangers to speaking in tongues, prophecy and healing. Her visit and subsequent visits changed the whole state of Christian affairs. She started the Glad Tidings Tabernacle which later became the Colombo Gospel Tabernacle under AOG Missionary Clifford.

The Ceylon Pentecostal Mission began in 1923, founded by Ramankutty, who was a Malayalam Hindu from Kerala, India. Later he was to be known as Pastor Paul. He came to Sri Lanka when he was just sixteen and worked for Azariah, who himself was a convert to Christianity.[3]

Ramankutty, at a time in his life, threw away the Bible that was given to him and avoided contact with Christians. Later, he had a vision of Jesus Christ who appeared to him and asked him to come and serve him. He did not tell anyone about this vision fearing he would be thrown out of his home. Later he publically testified to this life-changing experience. He joined the Church of Ceylon and was sent to Kottayam for theological training. When he returned, he was appointed the Catechist of the Malayalam Mission in Thimbirigasyaya. After he received Baptism in the Holy Spirit, he felt he could not remain in the Anglican church and resigned after much prayer and thought. Needless to say, he and his family embarked on a "Faith Mission", endured severe hardships.

His faithfulness and vision gave birth to the Ceylon Pentecostal Mission (CPM), which is one of the largest Pentecostal churches in the world. The CPM is also recognised as the first mission in a third-world country to send local missionaries to the West. They now have churches in 65 countries and over two million believers worldwide. The story of the AOG, the FFCSL, Foursquare and other independent churches is another story, and can be told at another time.

* * *

[2] *Ref: "Asian and Pentecostal: The Charismatic Face of Christianity in Asia"* edited by Allan Anderson, Edmond Tang

[3] *Ref:* http://www.pentecostmedia.com/PasPaul.htm

When he resigned from the Good Shepherd Church, my father was appointed by the CMS to be the Catechist/Pastor in place of Pastor Paul at the Malayalam Mission. My father knew him since both hailed from Kerala and both were out to serve the Lord. My father often spoke about Pastor Paul in endearing terms. Years later, I came to know Freddie, Sam and Harry Paul who became the Chief Pastors of the Mission. I was with Pastor Paul when he had a convention in France and I was surprised to notice that almost all the workers were of French ethnicity. About ten new believers were baptized that evening in a bathtub at the Faith Home! It is an amazing story of how a Hindu convert who was employed as a cook was chosen by the Lord to bring about a change in the Body of Christ in Sri Lanka and in Asia.

Before 1960, Pentecostalism survived outside the mainstream churches. Clergyman or laymen who claimed to have experienced the 'glossolalia' were politely tolerated or they left their churches and moved to others that were Pentecostal minded. If you were to ask when the Charismatic movement burst onto the world stage, it could be traced to the day when Dennis Bennet from St. Luke's Church in Seattle announced on television that he had spoken in tongues![4] It was as if a hurricane had made a landfall in Seattle. It caused some controversy but galvanized a positive reaction, since people in the mainline churches were hungry for more of God, than merely going through the rituals and liturgy of the church for years.

In Sri Lanka, up until 1960, healing, speaking in tongues and prophecy were associated with the fast growing Ceylon Pentecostal Movement. The CPM Pastors were celibate, churches were called Faith Homes. Pastors and full time sisters wore white and went two by two to witness. The people in the Faith Homes rose early in the morning at around 4.00 and prayed and praised the Lord. They had what is called a "tarrying meeting" where, for a prolonged time, those seeking baptism would be crying loud and this shouting and sound of the praising could be heard far and wide. A cardinal doctrine of the CPM was to live a consecrated life and that meant to be baptized by one of the CPM pastors, refrain from taking communion

---

[4] *Ref:* Larry Christenson (2002). "Bennett, Dennis Joseph (1917-91, and Rita (1934-)". In Stanley M. Burgess. *The new international dictionary of Pentecostal and charismatic movements.* (Rev. and expanded ed.). Grand Rapids, Mich.: Zondervan Pub. House. pp. 369–371. ISBN 0310224810.

in other churches and above all, refuse medicine when sick but trust the Lord for divine healing. The CPM also believed that they were the chosen 144,000 *(Rev. 7 and 14)* who would be admitted to Mount Zion.

We at this time began to receive the *Abundant Life* magazine of Oral Roberts, the *Faith Digest* of T. L. Osborn and the *Voice of Healing* monthly magazine. These magazines showed pictures of massive tent crusades and mass healing crusades in Ghana and Indonesia conducted by T. L. Osborn. The giant crusades were the result of the blind, deaf and the cripple being healed after prayer. Ninety percent of those who attended were non-Christians who were attracted to hear the Gospel because of these spectacular miracles, signs and wonders. We began to realize that in order to operate in such power we needed the endowment of power that Jesus promised his disciples. That endowment of power came upon them on the day of Pentecost when they were filled with power and began to speak with unknown tongues. The apostles performed mighty miracles in the name of Jesus and turned multitudes to Christ. So did the Apostle Paul who, by Word and Deed made them obedient to the Faith.

Our motif was to pray like Hannah for spiritual children to be born, to pray like Daniel against invisible powers, to intercede like Elijah for fire and spiritual rain. Week after week we called upon the Lord to send salvation to this nation.

On the 21st of November 1961, Ranjit De Silva told me, when we were getting ready for an open air service, that he received the baptism in the Holy Spirit. I asked him whether he spoke in tongues to which he answered in the affirmative.

On Friday the 24th, I was determined to pray the whole night to receive what I was longing for. Around three in the morning, while we were in prayer, I felt a sudden surge of power hitting me. The next thing I knew was someone was turning my tongue and then words like Chinese began to flow forth and continued for some time. The exhilaration and joy flooded my soul and I was thrilled that I had, at last, received what I had been praying for a long time. The intensity of the infilling and the subsequent joy that filled my heart, apart from a hundred spiritual rewards, the empowerment I received, has impacted and equipped me for the long years of ministry, both as Evangelist and Pastor. Those praying with me were Tissa Weeerasinghe, Sam Rajendran and Ranjit de Silva.

Needless to say, they were all excited and glad that I now too had been anointed by the Spirit and Tissa, a few weeks later was baptized in the Holy Spirit. We were all jubilant, convinced that this was the beginning of a new Pentecostal era for Sri Lanka.

I was baptized in the baptismal tank at Bethesda by Bruce Ker, with Jim Cook looking on. There had been some strong opposition from my parents to my decision to be baptized, but they eventually realized that I was sincere in obeying the Lord's teachings.

The news quickly began to spread widely and many who met us congratulated us for pressing on to receive the gift. Needless to say, the elders and believers knew sooner or later that these young men would experience the phenomena of the Spirit. We continued to worship and attend services as usual but made trips to estates and outstations to conduct our Gospel meetings.

In 1962, one of the Elders approached me and asked me whether I would be willing to serve as a Deacon, as Ron Hobbs was leaving the island and Fred Collette was on the brink of migrating to Australia. There was a condition attached to it. We young people must not speak in tongues within the church or pray for the sick during services, although it could be done while we were on Gospel Tours. I said I needed about two weeks to reply him as I needed to pray about this offer. Two weeks later I met the Elders and told them that my infilling of the Holy Spirit happened in that very room while we were praying, and I could not go against my conviction, so I would let the Deaconship pass by.

Except for Hobbs, the others accepted and sympathized with me on my stand. Shortly afterwards, we left the church and broke Bread in a private home for a few weeks. Needless to say, our remaining friends came and asked us to return to the church and promised that all would be well. We, however, thanked them and began to pray seriously for God's guidance regarding our collective future. We left an Assembly, long-time friends, precious believers and our loving mentors who had trained us in the Holy Scripture. There was a price to pay for renewal and revival.

The news of our Charismatic experience was viewed with alarm and unbelief by Bruce Ker and Jim Cook. These men were products of a

Seminary that was very conservative and felt that we were being sincerely misled by Faith Healers and Preachers from America.

Shortly after we received the experience of the Holy Spirit, Jim Cook was tipped off to authorities by a Christian brother that he had shot a deer at the Willpattu Nature Reserve. Immigration gave him fourteen days to pack up and leave the country. Bruce Ker, although he was not involved in the fray, also decided to return to America, immediately. It was a sad day when I went to his home and bade him farewell. In a sombre manner, not his usual style, he said, "Verghese, whatever happens, keep looking up to Jesus."

He and Jim Cook left the shores of this island with heavy hearts. They had done so much for the Body of Christ.

9

Move to the Biblical Free Church. Cloudburst of Revival Power. Out of the Corral. Galloping to the Four Corners of the Land for Christ.

The Bethesda Boys, as we were called, left the Bethesda Gospel Hall and began attending the Biblical Free Church (BFC) in Kirulapone during the later part of 1963.

The Biblical Free Church was an extension of the missionary work of the Swedes who had now come to Sri Lanka. Hannah Larson was in Colombo, Enar Stahre in Kandy and Bjokenforce in Nuwara Eliya from the Swedish Free Churches, and there was also Tommy Yrojala Captain of the Gospel Ship "Ebenezer" and Raul Laine from the Finnish Free Churches stationed in Sri Lanka.

As a woman, Hannah Larson was not permitted to hold any church office and serve Communion, and hence they found in Erik Nathanielz the ideal candidate to shepherd the fledgling new congregation. Hannah Larson was a missionary who always wore a warm smile and had a heartfelt love for children, who would cuddle them, especially if they were from poor families, and would invite them to the Sunday school.

Erik was a former pastor of the Ceylon Pentecostal Mission, who had resigned in 1945, the year Pastor Paul passed away. Erik was a powerfully built man, with booming voice and was a great singer. He knew almost all the songs in the Redemption Hymnal and even the tunes of the most obscure songs. His stature was tempered by a pleasing and winsome personality and he was known to have raised a boy from the dead during his tenure at the CPM.

More than any other missionary, Erik was gripped with the Sovereignty of the Local Church. Next to the Doctrines of Christ, as enumerated in the Book of Hebrews, Chapter 6, the independence of the local church seemed to be the most important rule or tenet for some of them.

Soon after we began to worship at the BFC, Bertil Steffanson decided to move to Colombo and began work with the BFC. Bertil had a genuine burden to see a revival in Sri Lanka. He invited Tage Sjoberg and his sons, Stanley and Stahre, to come and conduct revival meetings in the existing churches that were associated with Sweden. Tage was a towering figure but with a gentle and loving heart. Having lived in New York, he had a good command of the English language and, in retrospect, had a very fruitful ministry.

Bertil organized revival meetings in many churches, most of which I have mentioned before, and these brethren from the churches in Sweden came every year from 1963 to 1965 to minister, encourage and rejuvenate the believers. Although the main target of these conventions was to give a new lease of life to the churches, a number of people came and were saved, subsequently baptized and added to the churches.

I was invited to attend these conventions and then helped to pray with those who had come to the altar for salvation and filling of the Holy Spirit. I remember praying for several young people and the moment I laid my hands upon their heads they started to speak in new tongues. I was also asked to share short messages before Tage spoke. He would ask me to share, and with my Brethren background, my sermons appealed to many of the Pentecostals.

And so, I was at every convention and special meeting organized by Bertil during those years. The freedom to pray for people to receive baptism and witness their joy and jubilation afterwards was always fulfilling. We were able to pray and, on several occasions, able to cast out demons in the name of Jesus. When we saw people being converted, baptized and filled with the Holy Spirit, we were reminded of the prophetic words of the Apostle Peter who said "it shall come to pass in the last days *[eschatology]* says God, that I will pour out of My Spirit on all flesh; your sons and your daughters shall prophecy, your young men shall see visions, your old men shall dream dreams. And on My manservants and on My maidservants I will pour out My Spirit in those days; and they shall prophecy." *(Acts 2:17-18)*

We were now able to function without any constraints or limitations. We were free and out of the corral where sincere men had set up boundaries.

We had said our goodbyes to Bethesda, albeit with more than a tinge of sadness for leaving a group of faithful Elders and devoted members of the congregation. It was saddening to leave behind many of our younger friends.

* * *

We were now in a hall built wholly with galvanized metal sheeting. The walls, roofing and the sides were all made out of sheeted zinc. During the day it was sweltering and even the blessed coolness of a shower of rain was marred by the relentless '*RAT-TAT-TAT*' of rain on the tin roofing sheets drowning out the preacher's voice.

The hall was built on a rented piece of land at *Rubberwatte* (rubber estate) in Kirulapone. It was a far cry from the comfort we were used to at Bethesda. I remember my father relating how, early one morning at around half past five or so, cycling on his way to St. John's Church to conduct a service, he passed this rubber estate and nearly rode over a python that was trying to cross the road.

The BGH was situated in a top residential area and was a spacious hall with a large parking area and a lawn to play basketball or netball. It could seat easily nearly 300-350 people. There were large windows and spacious pews. The church was self-supporting and never appealed for any money.

In contrast, the BFC was a 50 x 30 foot hall with forty chairs, a wooden pulpit and a small organ that was played by Erik's daughter Dalrene. Our Sunday services at BGH had inspiring singing, music, and expository preaching and teaching by world class preachers. Now we listened to Erik who would tend to ramble along, yet produced some very useful insights which we did not easily forget.

At BGH, the services were orderly, organized and would end on time. Since Erik was trained at the CPM, he had a tendency to come unprepared for a service hoping the Spirit would provide the strategy. For a more in-depth understanding and analysis of the men and women who were a part of the BFC, read Professor Somaratne's book *"History of Calvary Church"*.[1]

Liberty of the Spirit must be combined with astuteness and perspicacity. Raul Laine, the Finnish Missionary, often said, "It's a big job for God to make a natural man spiritual and a bigger job to make a spiritual man natural again."

As soon as we joined the BFC, we were given numerous tasks: Ranjit was appointed as the Superintendent of the Sunday school and he did an admirable job at that. He was a good organizer and the result was increased attendance and a team of eager teachers. Tissa was assisting the church in its various departments, especially with the youth. We were soon joined by my brother, M. C. Mathew, and Hugh Kanagasabay. Both of them were holding worthwhile jobs, but resigned and came into the fulltime ministry.

Now that we were out of the corral, we began to plan out a strategy to reclaim territories where the rule of the Kingdom of God was barely evident. One such campaign was to the highlands of the island – Nuwara-Eliya.

Nuwara-Eliya is located in the central province at 5,600 feet above sea level. Nuwara-Eliya is called "Little England" because of its climate which is akin to England and much cooler than Colombo. The finest tea comes from tea plantations surrounding the town. The slopes of these hills look as if they are covered by a green carpet. These are tea bushes that are pruned by women tea pluckers almost every other day. The British began to plant these tea estates in the beginning of the 19th century.

The story of how tea came to Ceylon is most interesting. During the end of the 18th century, Britain was close to a revolution. Its people were poor and water was contaminated, so, people turned to alcoholic drinks such as whisky, ale and especially apple cider. Farmers would get drunk on gallons of apple cider, daily. This was becoming an uncontrollable epidemic.

At this time two brothers, Charles and John Wesley, began to preach

[1] *Ref:* G. P. V. Somaratna (2006) *"History of Calvary Church"*. Calvary Theological Seminary. ISBN 955-587-052-7

the Gospel throughout the British Isles. Their preaching created a huge spiritual revival and they abstained from these alcoholic or semi-alcoholics drinks. They now needed an alternative beverage and that came in the form of the Ceylon Tea! James Taylor was the first Scotsman to start planting tea in 1867. Britain bought most of our tea and even the Queen had her evening cup! The Methodist revival by the Wesleyan Brothers made Britain the first nation of tea drinkers. The spiritual revival changed the drinking habits of the British who came and planted tea in ever increasing numbers. Today, tea is one of the main sources of foreign exchange to Sri Lanka and, at one time, we were the largest exporters of tea. A spiritual Tsunami had its epicentre in Britain, but its waves were felt in a faraway island, popularly called Lipton's Tea Garden.

In order to reach the vast masses employed in these estates, we had to have the campaign in the centre of the town and also early in the evening, so that people could return home before dark.

During one of our outreach programs, I met Albert Jebanayagam from Jaffna. He had recently graduated from the Madras Christian University in Chennai, India with a B.A. degree. He had a passion for souls and had a haunting voice. Together we went to Nuwara-Eliya. The campaign was organized by Pastor Selvarajah and Margit Stefansson from Halsingborg, Sweden.

Albert led the song service. He was a master guitarist and the sprightly song service attracted people who had hardly any entertainment in the estates. The crowds increased each day and the campaign went on for eighteen days. We prayed for the sick, the wounded and the oppressed. People experienced the infilling of the Holy Spirit and a large number were converted and baptized. Believers braved the chilly rivers to be baptized, as the church had no interior baptismal tank. Among them were several who, today, are church leaders, both here in Sri Lanka and India. We would definitely not want to go back to the corral after what we saw, heard and experienced in Nuwara-Eliya.

Another one of our campaigns was held in the southern coastal city of Galle, at the Galle Town Hall and attended by a large number of non-Christians. T. L. Yrojola was the main Preacher. He was a hulky Finn with a commanding personality, yet easy smile. He was the captain of the

Gospel ship "Ebenezer" which arrived in Sri Lanka in 1956 with thirty Finnish men, women and children. It took the captain, his crew and their families over thirty days to traverse the seas to the Colombo harbour from Helsinki, Finland.

Yrojola was a missionary in China before the cultural revolution of 1949. He related an incident of visiting a woman who was a believer. By the time he got there he found that she had already passed away the previous night. She was young and Yrojala felt led by the Spirit to pray for her to return to life. He knelt down and prayed for some time. A while later, just as he had finished his prayer, she began to move and sat up, to the astonishment of all around her. She turned to the people around her and said, "Why did you bring me back? I was in Heaven!"

Years later, while the ship was anchored in Kayts, Yrojola felt a strong urge to go to Delft Island. Anchoring their boat, they walked to the closest village where they heard the sound of weeping and wailing. An elderly woman had died just a few hours earlier. Yrojola walked into the hut and began to pray. Then he commanded the dead woman to rise (Matthew 10:8 says "cure the sick and raise the dead"). Immediately she arose. Sitting up on her mat she declared, "O my God, I am glad you brought me back! I was in '*Naragam*' (hell). Thank you! Thank you!"

Many in the village, seeing these miracles, turned to the Lord that day. When he related these two incidents, a swell of people came to the front to receive Christ as Saviour and Lord. A young man stood at the back. I felt that it was his appointed day to receive salvation and was able to lead him to the front. Soosiri Liyanage is today a Pastor and has many churches under his supervision in many parts of the island.

10

State of the Church and Pastors – Mid-Sixties and Today. Resignation from Central Bank. My Mission as an Evangelist Begins. My Scriptural Letter of Appointment. The Miraculous Release of Foreign Currency for Travel. Operation Mobilization. My Tour of Sweden and Finland. Returning the Return Ticket. The Brown Envelope. Clash at Hyde Park. The Testimony of Richard Wurmbrand. My Scholarship to Bible School.

The state of affairs of churches, pastors, Christian leaders, their training, position, administrative facilities and the attitude of the man on the street towards the Christian church as a whole was different back in the mid-sixties, than they are today.

Knowing full well the drawbacks and the challenges and oppositions I would invariably face, I made up my mind to resign from my relatively secure position at the Central Bank of Ceylon, and plunge into fulltime ministry.

No church or organization, here or abroad, offered me any funding or livelihood. It was not a decision that I could make lightly and, before leaving, I decided to seclude myself away from the hustle and bustle of city life and spend time in fasting and prayer.

I knew Brother Daniel Selvaratnam from the Puwakpitiya Ebenezer Gospel Hall back in 1963 and had led him to Christ. It just so happened that Selvaratnam was the chief clerk at the Karandapone Tea Estate in Kegalle. What more secluded and peaceful place could you find than in

Pentecostal or Charismatic Pastors Then and Now

	Then – mid 1960s	Now - 2013
Church Roots	Few had a church to attend. Most pioneered their own church	Majority in established churches
Transport	On foot, by bus or by train	By van, cars or motorcycles
Education	JSC, SSC, ex-company clerks. Self-educated or short-term schools,	Diploma, B.TH, M.Div., Ph.D. LBC, CTS, AOG Bible Colleges
Church Premises	Rented	Owned buildings seating 1,000-4,000
Discrimination	Mild legislation against churches	Organised attack on churches
Public perception	respected by general public	Accused of foreign allegiance
Unity and collaboration	Visible unity and co-operation	Bi-partisan mentality
Overseas travel	Occasional	Frequent trips
Church Growth	By conversion	Conversion and transfers

the bungalow of a clerk in the middle of a sprawling tea plantation?

Selvaratnam welcomed me into his home and allowed me the freedom to pray and seek the Lord. He later became the pastor of the Ebenezer Assembly of God Church in Puwakpitiya.

During my time of prayer, I found myself deliberating on a passage of the Scriptures, 2 Timothy 4:5, where it says, "you be watchful in all things, endure afflictions, do the work of an evangelist, fulfil your ministry." *(2 Timothy 4:5)*

I had received my directive: "Do the work of an Evangelist" and this was the verification I needed to confirm my call and vocation.

I returned to Colombo and planned to send in my resignation papers. I was fully aware of the risk that I was about to take, leaving a well-paid secular job. However, I also knew that I was not the only person who had ever made a decision of this magnitude and forfeit.

I saw the footprint of Abraham, who, when God had called him, went forth with blind faith, not knowing where he was going, yet he did not trouble his mind over it. Moses, by faith left Egypt behind him and endured steadfastly, gazing on whom who is invisible *(Heb 11.27)*. Jesus left his parents and home at the age of thirty to fulfil his father's work as did all his Apostles. Francis of Assisi (1181) renounced his wealth and started preaching to the poor in France. Martin Luther (1518) left the Roman Catholic Church and left his footprint both in Europe and in the entire world, Sadhu Sundar Singh (1922) forsook his family and stepped out to preach the Gospel in India and Tibet. Bakht Singh (1945) also gave up his wealth and went to build over 600 Churches in India. Ramon Paul left all to follow Christ; the Mission he founded has now over two million people. Here I was, about to carry my cross and go out to serve Christ. I was the least of these servants that went before me.

When Jesus carried his cross Simeon came forward and helped Him to carry that tree. Likewise, when I started my journey, there were many "Simeons" who helped me to on the Way. Multitudes both here and all over the globe have helped me on my journey of faith; all through my life as a servant of God.

* * *

Soon after my return to Colombo, I made an appointment with the Assistant Controller of the Central Bank. I wanted to apply for foreign exchange in order to purchase a ticket to fly to London.

I told him that I had received an invitation to attend the Operation Mobilization Conference in England but he said funds could not be released for such purposes unless I had a letter of appointment; then it could be considered.

"I do have one," I told him.

"Please show it to me," he asked.

"My letter of appointment is found in the Bible, in the Gospel of Matthew, Chapter 28, Verse 19 and 20: *'Go and make disciples of all nations, baptizing them in the name of the Father and of the Son and of the Holy Spirit, teaching them to observe all things that I have commanded you; and lo, I am with you always, even to the end of the age.'*"

The Controller stared at me in silence and astonishment and then said, "Okay. Write that down and send it to me and I will see what I can do."

"Thank you, sir," I replied and walked out of his office. Over the next couple of days I drew up my application indicating my calling to be an evangelist to the world and sent it to him. A week later I was called to the Finance Ministry at the Old Secretariat to meet Mr. Wanninayake who was the Finance Minister at that time.

I went up to the fourth floor and showed the lady my letter of appointment. She asked me to sit down in the small waiting room at the end of the hall.

I was somewhat nervous and decided to read a magazine that I had brought along called *"The Voice of Healing"* published by Gordon Lindsay in Dallas. I read these words: "Jesus sent forth His disciples," That was it. Jesus was sending me forth, not anyone there. I stood up, facing the cubicle where I was supposed to go in for the interview and said in a slightly audible voice: "I command you to release my funds so that I can go to England in the name of Jesus." At that very moment I was asked to come into the room where a burly man sat, looking at my application.

"So you are the evangelist! Where do you want to go?"

"To England, and then on to Sweden," I answered, truthfully enough.

"What!" he snapped, "Sweden? That is a sinful country! Why go there?"

"Jesus Christ came to save sinners, including sinners in Sweden," I replied.

With an "Okay, okay, go and sit down," he waved me away.

Half an hour later, I was called to the counter where I was handed over a document of approval for foreign exchange Rs. 4,004 had been permitted. A travel allowance of three pounds and ten shillings! Expressing my thanks, I walked out of the building. I also got my exit visa with the purchase of the ticket.

Before my departure to London, the BFC gave me a farewell service. Later, on the day of my departure, several people came home to wish me good bye and also to pray. Among them were Erik and Hannah. My brother Mathew was now quite active and I felt relieved that he was around, in my absence. Several prayed and then Hannah closed in prayer. My mother told me years later, that when Hannah prayed, she heard the prayer spoken in English, in the Malayalam language! She told me that when she heard this rare phenomenon she knew I would be safe, and, return safe and sound.

I should mention that when I resigned from the Bank in June 1965, Ben Alexander tendered his resignation from the Ceylon Shipping Company and so did my younger brother Abraham Libertus.

While I was in London, I heard that Tissa Weerasinghe who was working at Brown & Company had also resigned. This was followed by the resignation of Ranjit De Silva from Carson Cumberbatch. I advised them to pray before rushing into it.

On September 26th 1966, my friends accompanied me to the airport and saw me off as I flew Air France first to Paris and then on to London. I checked into a hotel in Paris, where, even though I was assured by my travel agent that the stay was on the airlines account, the hotel itself said that I must pay. With the paltry sum I had with me, this was disheartening news. Fortunately, I had the number of Frank Williams who was in Paris attending the CPM convention. He came to the hotel, and to my great relief and joy took me to the Faith Home. I met Freddie Paul there for the first time and heard him preach. The sermon was interpreted in French.

That evening I placed one pound in the offering plate. This was my first seed planted in Europe – in Paris. Now I had two pounds and ten shillings and a return ticket to Sri Lanka.

The next day, I flew on to London and was picked up by Noel Muthunayagam whom I had led to the Lord in the same Church that Brother Daniel had been saved. Noel's brother took me to his home and I had a good Sri Lankan meal, and, felt quite fulfilled. In the evening he drove me to Honour Oak where the Operation Mobilization conference was being held. OM was founded by George Verwer. He was converted during Billy Graham's Madison Ave, Crusade in 1955.

I came into the conference centre around seven that evening and the service had already started. I decided to go straight to the hall and heard George Verwer speak. George was a slim man of average height but I realized that he was very much devoted to the task of carrying out the Last Commission.

There were around 300 young people from USA, Canada, England, Germany, India and several other countries. After the meeting, which ended at half past nine or so, I felt hungry and was waiting to have dinner.

There was no sign that dinner was going to be served, so I searched for the kitchen and found it empty. I asked someone who was cleaning the kitchen floor about dinner. He looked at me thoroughly surprised and said that they already had dinner at five o'clock! In Sri Lanka we usually have dinner after eight or even later. I went to bed that night quite hungry and sleepy.

The young men slept in a large room, tucking themselves into sleeping bags, lending me a spare, when they saw that I did not have one. The young people were friendly and happy to know I had come all the way from Sri Lanka. One young chap asked me whether I had hitchhiked to London from Sri Lanka for the conference, stating that he had done just that from Australia.

The next day we had to rise up early and do exercises on the lawn. It was Fall and very cold. We were given our work schedule and I was given the task of cleaning and washing a toilet. I had never cleaned someone else's toilet in my life outside our own toilet at home! While cleaning and mopping the floor, I wondered if I had made a big mistake leaving my home and coming to a strange country.

The next day, all new comers were told to give all that they had into a box and that it will be shared among others. OM's are to trust the Lord and not receive or keep any money to themselves. What could I do now? One pound was given in Paris and I decided to give the 10 shillings that I had with me. Now I was left with just 2 pounds sterling! The OM argument was that the spiritual revolution would begin in others when we were willing to forsake all and follow Christ.

In the evening there was group prayer, two by two and in a format that was not tedious. It was moving to hear young people praying with much passion for countries like Turkey and India.

I vividly remember the entire group of participants praying for a ship to take the Gospel to the nations of the world. The ship was at no small cost and the money needed was £80,000. I, too, fervently prayed that the funds would be released soon. Later, when touring Europe, I learned that the OM had bought a minesweeper, christening it the MV Logos. Seventeen years later, it sunk off the cost of Chile, but not before receiving seven million visitors over 250 ports of call in 102 countries.

Around the same time in London, Frank Williams and I went to Hyde Park to the Speakers Corner. Hyde Park is one the famous Parks in London with an extent of over 350 acres and 4,000 trees. It has been a venue for numerous Rock Concerts. I had heard Billy Graham preach inside this park with hundreds of people raising their hand to accept Christ after a powerful Sermon.

There is a spot in Hyde Park called the Speakers Corner where anyone can come and stand on a footrest or chair and speak on any subject, although however, no one is permitted to speak against the Queen of England.

Armed with a lot of tracts and booklets, Frank and I went to this spot and began distributing pieces of literature. Soon a number of people gathered and I began to give Gospel Message reminding them that Jesus is the answer to all their needs. I also talked about repentance and faith in God.

As we continued speaking, the numbers began to increase and soon we were being heckled, interrupted and jeered at by some. When we continued speaking, the crowd began to hoot. They tried to shout me down. I vividly remember one English woman thrusting the tip of her umbrella at our faces and some others shouting back, "your Jesus is not the answer." One man shouted out in a loud voice, "Communism is the answer! That will solve all our problems!"

As the man spoke these words, a tall, pale-faced man came to where we were standing and began to speak. He wore a suit and looked to be about 60-65 years of age. He said, "Listen friends, do not talk about communism. I know what communism is. I have been in the Rumanian Prison. The way he rolled his "r"'s betrayed his Eastern European accent. He continued, "I have been in the Russian Prison for four..*rr*..teen years. I did not see the sun, the flowers, the moon or the snow as I was locked in. On my back are the maa..*rr*..ks of the beatings I suffered in prison. But in the prison I saw the face of Jesus. I know what Communism is and what it can do to man. Jesus was with me and I know He lives and He is the Saviour!"

There was pin drop silence. No one said a word after that. One by one they began to disappear. We were now left alone. The man put his hand on my shoulder and asked where we were from. I told him we were from Ceylon, as Sri Lanka was called back then. What mission are you from?

We are Charismatics. He looked at me and said, "I too know of the gifts of the Spirit," and walked away. There was no need to ask his name since we had heard that Richard Wurmbrand who wrote the book, *Tortured for Christ*[1], was in London. We were so thrilled to see him in person and beyond that, like an angel he came to our rescue and then walked away. What a testimony. No sermon could have convinced them about the nature of Communism and about the Truth.

Richard Wurmbrand was of Jewish descent and was imprisoned for the second time in Rumania for stating that Christianity is incompatible with Communism. His book *Tortured for Christ* became a bestseller and has been translated into sixty languages. He passed away in 2001.

* * *

Aina Andersson worked alongside us at the Biblical Free Church (BFC) for a short period of time before returning to Sweden. I informed her that I was planning to visit Sweden and whether she could arrange some meetings for me. I travelled by ship from London and arrived in Gothenburg on the west coast of the country. As the ship sailed towards the Arctic Sea I noticed icebergs adrift. Arriving at harbour, I was met by Aina and Mrs. Gottfridson. I was to be the guest of Gottfridson until meetings were planned elsewhere. The branches of the trees were all bare and with snow all around me, I felt a sinking feeling of hopelessness. What was left of my paltry allowance was diminishing by the day and except for one meeting in London there was no firm appointment.

Once snow fell throughout the night and when I awoke that morning and looked out of the window I saw a carpet of snow on the ground. Being my first experience with snow, I went outside and scooped some up, surprised that it melted so quickly in my hands.

The house was warm and I spent many days now in prayer and fasting. Sunday came and Mrs. Gottfridson told me we would go to church that evening. Donning myself with a warm coat I had picked up from the OM back in England, I got ready for my first church service in Sweden. The coat, which looked like the kind soldiers used in the Second World War,

---

1 *Ref:* Richard Wurmbrand (1940.6.1) *"Tortured for Christ"*. Crossway Books. ISBN 034-086-368-4

hung down to my ankles fastened in the front with huge buttons.

The church was called Gilead and was part of the Free Churches of Sweden. This was one of the 700 Pentecostal Churches of Sweden with their history dating back to 1913. The largest of them, with a 3,000-strong membership, was the Filadelfia Church in Stockholm founded by Pastor Lewis Petrus.

Since the expulsion of the Filadelfia Church from the Baptism Church of Sweden, the most dominant issue was the independence of the local Church; an issue that continued to be debated for decades.

The Filadelfia Church was the flagship of the SPC. It had a capacity to hold 3,000 people and was, back then, the largest church in Europe. They had a fleet of missionaries around the globe. The Churches in Oslo, Helsinki, Copenhagen, Hamburg and Frankfurt were inspired by this iconic Church founded by Lewis Petrus.

The Gilead Church, itself was located in the suburb of Gothenburg, the second largest city in Sweden. The service was in Swedish and when the singing ended the offering plate was sent around. There was no song leader and the pastor started the song while the congregation followed. The songs were from a hymn book similar to the Redemption Hymnal.

I sat there in deep thought. This was the first time I was attending a service at a Swedish Church. Where was I going next? Stanley Sjoberg had told me to wait until he organized meetings for me. I then remembered the words of Jesus, 'If anyone comes to me and does not hate his father and mother, wife and children, brothers and sisters – yes, and his own life also – he cannot be My disciple. And whoever does not bear his cross and come after Me cannot be My disciple.' *(Luke 14:26-27)*

I had a few Swedish Kroners with me and before I could think of what I would do, found the offering bag dangling in front of me. I took all the currency notes I had and shoved it into the red bag. I still remember the colour of that bag into which I gave all that I had.

Monday, the following day, I was free to pray. I went for a brisk walk and scrambled up a hill overlooking the meadows and fields. There on that hill in Sweden, I sang out loud that popular song, *"How Great Thou Art"*. I had first heard that song, composed by Carl Gustav in 1885 to the melody of a Swedish folk song, at the SCM conference when the group from Nagaland sang it.

A thought in the form of a question came to me: *"Can you really trust Me unconditionally and utterly?"* I searched my heart to see if I had forsaken all that I had and was now following the Lord. I remembered my return ticket tucked away in my suitcase. I had held onto it carefully in case I had to return to Sri Lanka. I decided then and there that I would post it to my brother who could get a refund from the travel agent.

With some apprehension, I posted that letter carrying the precious return ticket and now I had done what my Master had called me to do. Anxiety turned to a supernatural peace that flooded my soul with an assurance that all would be well.

The following day, Lizzie Gottfridson said we would go to the Smyrna Church in Gothenburg and later to the railway station to buy my ticket to Stockholm. I took my winter coat from the rack, shrugged it on and told her that I was ready to go. I was very averse to telling her that I had no money for the ticket. We drove to the church and attended the evening service. At the church, I met Margaretha Robberforce who worked as a nurse in Hatton and also attended our services. She hurried up to me and declared, "I have an envelope for you, please take it."

It was a brown envelope, which I received and thanked her for. On the way to the station, I sat in the car and opened the envelope to see what it contained. To my great surprise disbelief there were 200 Kroners inside – more than what I needed for my ticket! I was in tears as I knew this was from the Lord who so graciously provided for me at the last hour. Deep within me there was a solid affirmation that I will never be without help in the future.

The next day, I arrived at Stockholm and stayed with a family called the Pearsons. Their eldest son, Bengt, spoke English fluently and made me feel at home. Here I met Stig Anthin, a former missionary to Sri Lanka and whom I had met in Kandy in 1964.

From Stockholm, I went to Helsinki, Finland, where I was the guest of T. L. Yrojola for a few weeks. I travelled with him to Tampere and several other places sharing testimonies of what the Lord had done. It was now the peak of winter and the roads were covered with snow and ice. On one occasion the train was unable to proceed due to heavy snow on the tracks.

I spoke at the largest Pentecostal church, Saleem, in Helsinki and returned to Stockholm and travelled to many churches in Sweden.

In June 1966, I made a short trip to Norway and travelled with Haga, a veteran Norwegian missionary, to Japan. I remember preaching in the streets of Oslo at half past ten at night. It was still light enough to read the Bible and see the people standing before you.

As I stepped off the train at the Oslo station, I heard that a war between Israel and Egypt had broken out. When the six-day war ended, Israel had captured Jerusalem and re-occupied it after 2,000 years! Jesus had predicted that Jerusalem shall be trodden down by the Gentiles until the end of time or before he returns back to the earth.

In Norway I met an affable and friendly brother called Christianson who told me there was a Bible School in England where he had studied and recommended it to me. Thus, I first heard of the International Bible Training Institute in Brighton, England. I applied for admission, with the only recommendation being the letter from Pastor Erik of BFC. They had sent a letter back offering me a scholarship.

11

Prayer Partner Dieter Kemesi. Itinerating in Germany. The Miraculous Healing of Body and Spirit of Andreas Schwabe. Meeting Hildegard Schwabe. Neo-Pentecostalism. The Jesus Movement and Eastern Mysticism. The Spirit Moves at St. Margarets.

On my trip to London in 1967, armed with my letter for scholarship to Bible College, I was met by Jacob Perera. Jacob had conducted extensive evangelistic meetings in Scandinavia. His faith messages were well received in churches everywhere. He drove me to Brighton where the International Bible Training Institute (IBTI) was located. The IBTI was founded by Fred Square, an Evangelist. He had felt the burden to establish a Bible Training Centre especially for young Europeans whose churches had suffered during the war years. There were students from the UK, Germany, India, Kenya and several other nations.

I happened to be the first Sri Lankan to study at IBTI. I was followed by my bother Libertus and then several others from Sri Lanka. It was at IBTI that Libertus met Iremali from Finland, and when they graduated, they got married. After a while in Finland, Libertus and Iremali left for Sri Lanka and established eighteen churches in the Kandy area, especially along the Mahaweli River banks.

At IBTI, I came to know Dieter Kemesis from Germany. He was a fun-loving, yet strong, spiritual prayer warrior. I found in him a steadfast and reliable prayer partner. We used to pray inside the Glass House, a greenhouse where they grew vegetables during winter. There was also

Prabudas Vasu from India, whose father was the pastor of the Madras Pentecostal Church in India. Dieter and I made plans to travel to Germany together and he would be my interpreter.

Soon after graduation, we began our itinerary from Hannover. He was a member of the BFP which had churches mostly in the north. He planned meetings in those churches and the last meeting was to be held in Reutlingen. His sister was a member of the Volksmission Church which was pastored by Rudy Schwabe, the brother of Hildegard.

It was winter when we arrived in Reutlingen and in the crisp, cold weather, we began the week-long series of meetings. I was the first Sri Lankan to ever preach in this church and we were warmly welcomed.

The Volksmission Church in Reutlingen was pioneered by Andreas Schwabe and his family. In earlier times, he was both a free thinker and a chain smoker who had lost a lucrative business during the war in Bessarabia (now called Moldavia) where many Germans migrated and were settled, after the black plague.

When war broke out and the news came to their village, they had fled by night on horse-drawn wagons, hoping to reach the northern part of Germany. Along the way, Hildegard, who was less than a year old, died and plans were made for her burial. Her mother, however, vehemently refused and said that they would wait till they got to the other side of the river Weichsel, bundling her in warm blankets and keeping her close in her arms. Crossing the river, to their great amazement and joy, they saw a flicker of life in the baby.

Andreas and the family were settled temporarily by the German Government in Northern Germany, Marne being the closest Town. His wife Ida loved music and was attracted by some Christian songs in the neighbourhood. She began attending weekly meetings where she accepted the Lord to become a true Christian.

The eldest son, Rudolf, heard a group of people singing and sharing how God had changed and brought meaning into their lives. He and his friend Kurt decided to follow the invitation to them to attend the church meeting. Right there, both accepted the Lord as their Saviour, and as Rudy has mentioned many times, a great peace and joy filled their hearts.

Andreas was agreeable to his wife going to some kind of religious meetings, but certainly not his children. He told Rudy that religion was for the weak and for those who could not manage their own lives and needed someone to hold on to. There is no God.

Sometime later, Andreas experienced an excruciating pain. He would rest on the sofa and hold his stomach tightly with one hand, the cigarette in the other, being a chain smoker who could not bring himself to quitting the habit however much he tried to. Consulting the only doctor in the area, he was told that he had a torn diaphragm and needed immediate surgery which was rather dangerous at that time. His physician, Dr. Ring, advised him to make his last will. On the operation table Andreas spoke to God asking him to be merciful and spare his life, and that he would follow him and stop smoking. (He had thought, that would be his biggest sacrifice and therefore would be very pleasing to God.)

The believers in the church prayed fervently for Andreas. The surgery was a success and soon he was able to return home to continue living his former life. He had no interest in spiritual matters until one day he began to experience again, the pain in his stomach. The doctor, shaking his head in dismay, revealed that the former tear was opening up again and he needed further surgery, adding that the second surgery would be more critical.

Obviously shaken to hear this diagnosis, Andreas had told the surgeon that he would consult another doctor. Mildly upset, Dr. Ring reminded him that there was no other doctor. "I'm the only one! If you think He can help you," he said, pointing at the sky, "Forget it. He doesn't exist!"

Andreas began to pray in earnest, and the pain subsided. The tear had healed itself. He never needed another surgery.

This miraculous healing was the turning point in his life and he now became a very devout believer and encouraged the whole family to attend church. This was the man who, earlier on Sunday mornings, would let the air out of the tires of the bicycle and hide the pump to prevent them from going to church. But they would walk, even though the church was some distance away from their house. Now he bought a small car and crammed it with his family and anyone else who would come to church. While the whole nation was still reeling from the aftermath of the Second World War, Andreas and his family found Grace in the sight of God.

* * *

Dieter and I would pray every morning and preach in the evenings. After the service we would be surrounded by a number of young German girls who were keen to talk to us, some trying to practice their English whilst others were keen to know about Ceylon. The pack of girls was led by Hildegard, since she spoke better English than the others. Hildegard was a fresh-faced young lady, whose outgoingness was easily noticed. When we were invited to lunch at her father's house where we were treated to a delicious German meal, Hildegard was a gracious host.

DK and I decided to sing a song in German for the evening service and chose the song *"Burdens Are Lifted At Calvary"*. I remember Hildegard quickly sat down and translated that song into Germany. She was full of life and so energetic. When I bade them farewell, she saw me off outside the gate at Bloomen Strasse and I felt a twinge in my heart. I wondered whether this would be the girl that I would marry one day.

As soon as I arrived in London, I sent her a recording of the Great Hymns sung in Billy Graham's crusade. Her reply was prompt, thanking me for the gift. Since I was leaving for the USA I thought it best to correspond with her by mail. We did this while I was in the USA and we gradually became romantically involved, even though thousands of miles separated us.

I of course saw no problems, even though we were from vastly different cultures. During the time we were separated, both of us spent much time in prayer. Her church was keen to send her to Africa as a missionary but in her heart of hearts, she knew it would be Asia.

* * *

In 1968, I flew into America from England and at the New York airport I was asked at Immigration, "Young man, what brings you to America?"

I replied, "I am an evangelist."

He looked up at me and said, "Oh, not another Billy Graham!" stamped my passport and sent me off with a smile.

1968 was the defining year for America and the World. Martin Luther King was assassinated in Memphis and B. Kennedy in Los Angeles. It was also the year when the winds of the Charismatic movement were blowing strongly and powerfully across America.

From the US, I crossed over to Vancouver, British Columbia in Canada – a most beautiful city by the sea with blue mountains in the distance. It had a perfect climate right throughout the year, being close to the sea.

I visited St. Luke's Church in 1968 and saw a number of nuns raising their hands and praising God. The atmosphere was bathed in love and people from so many denominations were expressing their love and affection to each other in prayer. Jesus prayed for his people to be united in love and here it was tangibly manifested.

A fresh wind of the Holy Spirit began to blow and the dead bones in the mainline churches began to receive new life. American Lutheran minister Harold Bredesen, in 1962, coined the word "charismatic" and went on to describe the movement as the beginning of "Neo-Pentecostalism", although he preferred to call it "the charismatic renewal in the historic churches".

I stayed with David Dharmaratnam who hailed from Panditheruppu in Jaffna. He used to be boarded in Colombo. Back then, we had an open air service on the pavement in front of the Wellawatte Methodist Church. Soon after, a group of people gathered to hear us sing and preach. The crowds used to mainly consist of Buddhists who were curious to watch a group of young people practicing their religion outside the church, while they themselves were reluctant to perform their *pooja* or rituals outside of their clean and well-swept temples, especially in a place where people walk and move about.

We had by now, a good number of people surrounding us and listening. Among them was David. When the altar call was given, he came forward and was prayed for in public. We took his name and address and I visited him at his boarding house. Later I invited him to come to our Biblical Free Church (now Calvary Church) and while praying together on the cement floor, he suddenly began to shout "Hallelujah!" and speak in new tongues. He could barely keep quiet. When he calmed down, there was a glow on his face. "Brother, brother!" he said, "I saw Jesus. He was wearing a red robe and looked at me with such love!"

Later he migrated to Canada, and here I was, staying at his apartment. David was now attending St. Margaret's Episcopal Church. This was a church now leading the Charismatics. Pastor Birch received the Baptism in the Holy Spirit and the normal service was now fully packed with older people and visitors from all over Vancouver. I was surprised to notice that the services were unstructured and there was manifestation of singing in tongues as well as prophecy. This was the first time I had heard a whole congregation singing in tongues.

What had surprised me was to see scores of hippies enjoying the singing and the worship. Several of them had waist length hair, beards, and beads, dressed in multi-coloured clothing. A few looked like Jesus himself with their blond hair and beards, just like in some of the paintings of Jesus.

These young people were part of the Jesus Freaks or the Jesus People Movement. They surfaced after the Vietnam War and began to search for "Spirituality". They were disenchanted with traditional churches and frowned upon their wealthy parents, since their riches were not able to satisfy their inner longings.[1]

At this same time, Eastern Mysticism and psychedelic drugs exploded on the scene. Maharishi and Hare Krishna movements were gathering momentum.

Now, here was a movement that had the supernatural element as they were speaking in strange unknown languages that were out this world. Speaking in tongues gave them a feeling of love, power and joy. In the Charismatic Church, all were one in Christ. Many of them lived in communes and when they came to Church it was a bigger commune with lots of people loving and caring for them.

The Charismatics overhauled the worship service of churches with choruses based on the Word, and a host of new worship songs was on overhead projectors. Hymns books disappeared as people now looked at the screen and were able to raise their hands in worship and praise. This revolution was exactly what the Jesus People wanted and the Charismatics gave it to them. The operation of prophetic and healing gifts provided the supernatural element they were otherwise seeking in Hare Krishna and Maharishi and, of course, in drugs.

When I was at St. Margaret's, Dr. Calvin Chambers from the First Presbyterian Church met me and invited me to work at his church. He

[1] *Ref:* David Di Sabatino (1999) *"The Jesus People Movement: An Annotated Bibliography and General Resource"* (Westport, CT: Greenwood Press)

was longing to see a move of the Spirit in his own church. I joined Calvin and Alice in prayer regularly, and on one occasion, he too began to speak in tongues. Soon I noticed a great release in Calvin and the next week, at Wednesday service, he announced that ten years earlier, he had received the baptism of the Holy Spirit, but had never spoken to anyone about it.

Soon the services began to look like St. Margaret's, with lots of praise and worship. People flocked in to see what was going on. This was a church of mostly upper class parishioners with many businessmen among them. Much joy was now evident as people loved coming to the church.

I had to leave for Sri Lanka at the end of 1969 and was glad I was used as the mid-wife to bring forth the Charismatic baby to the Westminster Church. Dr. Calvin and Alice became very close and they have been wonderful friends to us over the years. He is now retired. David lives in Vancouver and continues to pastor a church in the city.

While I was still in Vancouver, preparing to return to Sri Lanka, I was at my last meeting at Kingsway Foursquare Church. Its Pastor, John Holland, asked me what I planned to do when I returned to Sri Lanka. I told him and the congregation that I was hoping to establish a bible school in Sri Lanka as there was no functioning bible school in the island at that time.

12

Back to Sri Lanka. BFC Moves to New Premises. Beginning of the Lanka Bible College. The First Principal. Stig Anthin and Herbert Mjorud Housed at Lighthouse Church. Our Wedding at Calvary. The Beginning of the Che Guevara Rebellion. A Headache and a Miraculous Save. Sirisena Finds the Grace of God. The 'Jeevana Ganga' Ministry. The Miraculous Release of Property by Presidential Decree. LBI Moves to the Former Hebron School. Don Allen, Christ for the Nations and the Bible School.

On our journey back to Sri Lanka, we had, along with Mjorud, scheduled meetings in Roma, Bombay, Madras and Colombo. While transiting at the Bombay Airport, we ran into Stig and his wife Majken. Quite surprised by this unexpected encounter, I asked them where they were going. Stig replied, "We are going to Sri Lanka to start a Bible School."

I was elated. "This," I told him, "is also my vision – to start a Bible school. We must get together once we arrive."

The Swedish Missionaries who arrived in Sri Lanka in the early sixties, not only conducted revival meetings but also held "short-term" Bible Schools in Kandy. The Lighthouse Church, being centrally located in the hill city of Kandy, also had the provision to afford lodging for prospective students. These courses were offered from 1963 to 1965. In 1965, Stig Anthin from Sweden, was the main teacher of the school. Stig, who had been an engineer before he became a missionary and Pastor, had a good command of the English language, and, was a good preacher.

I had returned to Sri Lanka in January 1970, after nearly three and a half years. We moved the Biblical Free Church from the galvanized tin shed to a rented facility, meant to have been a film studio. The new address: 31 Siebel Avenue, Kirulapone. It had a large hall amongst other facilities and the Church was renamed the Calvary *Devasthanya*[1].

The new leadership was young and dynamic and Kanagasabay was a remarkably brilliant preacher. He reminded me of that famous Methodist Preacher, Dr. D. T. Niles. Pastor Mathew had his grip on the affairs of the church and I enjoyed preaching on Sundays.

The three of us paid rent for the upper floor, while the church undertook to part pay the rent. The day we pulled down the old zinc sheets and carried them away to stock them in the garage at Siebel Avenue, was indeed a happy day.

The services had a new format. The old Redemption Hymnal was stored in the Library and a new Hymn book with Scripture chorus was printed. The new building where the congregation gathered for worship, prayer and other activities did have an influence of on the well-being of the church. New people felt comfortable in the larger preaching hall with fans and large windows. It could accommodate around 130-150 people. Christie Khoban was now with us at Calvary and he interpreted the messages into Sinhala.

We built a baptismal tank in just two days and baptized the first convert, Bella, who later became the Secretary of the Church.

With the move, came a sense of elation, for we were now well founded to plan future prospects and carry on, full steam ahead with our mission.

That was the time when I was informed that Anthin and some Brethren were coming to meet me to discuss the possibility of starting the Bible School. At that meeting held in the new church building, I presented a "White Paper" outlining our purposes, plans and suggestions for the curriculum, the recruitment of staff, *etc.* The Brethren were very pleased and unanimously voted to appoint me as the Principal. The school now had a name – The Lanka Bible Institute.

In Germany, Hildegard was happy that my vision to start a Bible school

[1] *'Devasthanaya'* means 'Church' in Sinhala

was becoming a reality so soon. Since there was no functioning Bible School, they knew what an important step this meant for the country and they prayed in Germany for us.

Later I realized that both Mathew and Hugh were disappointed that I had decided to leave Colombo and settle down in Kandy. Again a decision was made which meant I would leave my parents, family members, friends whom I had known for many years, and relocate to Kandy in the hill-country. My destiny for the next thirty years was sealed. I loved the salubrious climate of the up-country, the sprawling tea estates, the winding roads along the mountains, the icy water showers in the mornings and the cool evenings when mist covered the town.

* * *

Anthin and I met frequently in his rented house behind the Lighthouse Church on Piachaud Lane which overlooked the entire city and the lake. We discussed the syllabus and who could be potential teachers. Apart from Anthin, Stahre, Moses and myself, we decided to invite Ranjini Jayakrishna who had just graduated from Birmingham Bible College and Susantha Dissanayake, a graduate from The Assembly of God Bible College in Bangalore. Nagendran (now Dr. Chara) was to teach Health Care and Mr. Subasinghe, the 'schoolmaster' to teach Sinhala. He was the only teacher who wore the national dress.

We had the inaugural ceremony of the Lanka Bible Institute (LBI) on the 10th of September 1970 with great joy and jubilation. There were twelve students when we began. There were students from Lighthouse, Calvary Church, Smyrna from Nuwara-Eliya, New Life Centre from Colombo and a few others. Some were freshly saved and expressed high commitment to serve the Lord. On the inaugural day, during the time of Praise and Worship, one of the new students was filled with the Holy Spirit, a confirmation that the Father was pleased with our endeavours.

In 1970 I was part of the Mjorud Evangelistic Association (MEA). Mjorud was delighted that I was appointed the Principal of the Lanka Bible Institute.

Although I was Principal, I was not on a salary. The MEA was completely in agreement with my plans and purposes for the school. The school was now housed at the Lighthouse Church premises. We gave a salary to two staff members, Ranjini and Susantha. The cook Ariyadasa was also paid. Ariyadasa was working for us at Calvary Church but when I moved to Kandy, he too decided to come and work at the LBI.

The MEA not only supported me financially but agreed to help with the monthly budget of the LBI. Funds to run the school also came from Swedish Churches through the sponsorships of Anthin and Stahre.

Partnership in the Mission is so important. The Kingdom of God and his rule would spread outward and swell if churches and Missionary organizations are willing to serve without fanfare, even if their names are not prominently displayed on church boards. When Jesus called Peter and said 'come and follow me,' the rest of the fisherman joined Peter because Peter was following Jesus, even though Jesus did not mention any of them by name. The clash of missionaries and the nationals happens, because of the undue importance demanded for by the sending church or mission. Pastor Paul of the CPM and George Verwer of the OM founded huge organizations that are girdling the globe. Yet these two men shunned publicity. Pastor Paul, they say, shook his body so that they would not be able to get a good high definition shot of him. In all the OM publications you will hardly find a photo of Verver. These men understood what John the Baptist said, "He must increase, but I must decrease". *(John 3:30)*

Mjourd was an attorney-at-law who resigned and became a Lutheran Pastor. He was baptized in the Holy Spirit and began his own Evangelistic organization. He loved the Body of Christ and travelled to many nations to preach and pray for the sick. He had a special gift to help people to receive the Holy Spirit. When Mjorud saw the progress we were making at LBI, he kept the financial support going. He visited Sri Lanka every year and we organized Renewal meetings for him and his team.

In 1974, we convened a Charismatic Conference in Kandy and had it at the Fathima Catholic Retreat Centre. We had scores of Priests and Nuns attending this Retreat and many were baptized in the Holy Spirit. Fr. Jayamanne, who headed the Catholic Renewal movement, was also present at these meetings in Kandy.

* * *

We celebrated our wedding on February 24th 1971. Hildegard had arrived less than two months in Sri Lanka when we had our wedding. Stig Anthin solemnized the marriage and Frank Williams gave the homily. Emmanuel Jayakrishna and Nulun De Alwis (*nee* Weerasinghe) were the Best Man and Bridesmaid. A local group called The Sunbeams provided the music and singing.

Frank Williams was a businessmen, a friend of our family and an energetic leader who started the New Life Centre, bringing many young people to the Lord. He spoke from the Book of Ruth, reminding us that Ruth, when given a choice, said to Naomi, her mother-in-law, "For wherever you go, I will go... your people shall be my people and your God, my God." *(Ruth 1:16)* A very apt passage as Hildegard would now live and work among a people she did not know.

The students of the Lanka Bible School had a guard of honour for us as we entered the church. A number of believers from Lighthouse Church were also present and took part in the service. This was the first wedding officially conducted in the church and our names are the first on the wedding register at Calvary Church, Kirulapone.

We spent a few days in Negombo after our wedding and returned to Kandy on the 27th of February 1971. We came back in time for special renewal meetings in Kandy held by the preacher Herbert Mjourd, a former Attorney and Lutheran Minister from Minnesota, USA.

On the 4th of April 1971, Hildegard and I decided to travel to Colombo to visit my parents, and friends who had given us presents for our wedding. We usually stayed a night over and returned to Kandy the next day. That evening, we went to Galle Buck near the Lighthouse and watched the sunset over the Indian Ocean. While the sun was setting, the sky was a riot of red and orange colours. Looking back, I wonder, was that setting sun with red spirals a presentiment of the setting of the age of innocence and the dawning of an era of unprecedented and unending violence in this Emerald Isle?

All of a sudden, Hildegard told me she was not feeling too well and that she had a severe headache. She suggested that we return to Kandy the same night. Cancelling all other plans we drove back to Kandy around eight that evening and reached home by 10.30 pm. The journey to Kandy is along lush paddy fields and the closer to Kandy you get it becomes alpine and cooler.

The next morning we went to the Lighthouse church at 502 Peradeniya Road to talk to friends there. The news of attacks on police stations by insurgents (Che Guevara rebels) began to trickle into Kandy. As we were engaged in earnest conversation, Enar Stahre and his wife, Rachel, drove up and parked their yellow Volvo under the porch. Both scrambled out of the car, their faces pale and pallid. They had gone through some nerve-racking experiences and they were bursting to share it with us.

They had left Kandy that morning, the 5th of April, for Colombo, on some errand. As they had approached Warakapola, a lonely stretch of road snaking through paddy fields, men had stood in the middle of the road, signalling for them to stop. As they had slowed down and pulled off to the side of the road, more of the men had come and surrounded the car. On noticing that they were foreigners, the young men had called somebody on their walkie-talkie and spoken for a while. Enar and Rachel were frightened, not knowing what would happen to them. Rachel began to speak in tongues and the men asked Enar where he was going. He replied, "Colombo."

"Go back, go back! You cannot go any further – the roads are closed."

Slowly he reversed his car and circled back onto the Kandy Road. The moment they were on their way, they had raced back to Kandy, their Volvo almost flying.

Hildegard and I would have encountered these insurgents had we left for Kandy that morning as we had originally intended, and possibly would have been held up somewhere along the way. The loving Grace of God protected us from the first day of the April Insurgency by triggering that headache which disappeared the next day. The Stahre's were protected in the midst of a very unsafe and a dangerous situation. We all stood around each other and thanked the Lord profusely for Grace bestowed upon us in the midst of great terror.

The next day, an island-wide curfew was imposed, and we could not leave our homes. The only news we were able to get was from the radio since there was no TV at that time. Every evening we turned into the Commercial Service of Ceylon and heard very demoralizing and dismal news. The insurgents had attacked several police stations and killed many security personnel. They had even planned to kidnap the Prime Minister but were foiled in their attempt. The Indian army was asked to come and help the local police and the next day, a contingent of Sikh soldiers with their turban and beard were pictured arriving at the Airport. They had taken up position guarding vital installations. The curfew lasted over the next few days and was temporarily lifted only for a few hours daily, allowing people to go out and buy provisions.

The Che Guevara Movement, as it was called, was named after Che Guevara who was a Bolivian Communist leader. He was a fierce fighter who believed in using violence to overthrow existing governments and replace them with a Marxist regime. He was the inspiration to our insurgents, to mount an attack on the Government, by force.[2]

The local Revolutionary movement was inspired and led by Rohana Wijeweera who studied in the Lumumba University in Moscow. The movement was composed mostly of unemployed and thus, frustrated Sinhala youth. Their aim was to seize power by force and establish a Socialist Government like in China and Russia. Wijeweera succeeded in training thousands of youth, especially from the countryside. They were given five lessons which talked about the crisis of the Capitalistic Government, Indian expansion, and the path of the Revolution. To achieve this goal, no quarter was given. They were taught that only by unbending violence and struggles would their goal be accomplished.

The days and weeks of April were spent mostly indoors. Hildegard and I were now married less than two months and we lived in Mapanawatura in the house of Mr. Tuwan Bongso who was a DIG[3] at that time. His house was built on a hill and we could see as far as the Knuckles mountain range and also the Katugastota Road. At night we heard sporadic gun shots which we assumed were the army battling the mutineer's. Despite the surrounding tension, we were however happy to be together after having been so long apart. We were able to pray, plan and go for small walks along the road leading to the main road.

We were not obliged to visit anyone nor was anyone able to come and visit us, due to the curfew and lack of transport. We often heard the

[2] *Ref:* Gamini Samaranayake, *"Political Violence in Sri Lanka, 1971-1987"*

[3] DIG: Deputy Inspector General of Police

sound of a police or army jeep driving past the road below our house. Hildegard was not only a stranger to the country, church and to the hill city of Kandy, but also to the turmoil and violence that was unleashed by the insurgents. She, however, remained very calm and was confident that God's protection was over us.

She had a vivid vision before she left Germany which she had shared with her close friend and prayer partner Renate Knecht, that Sri Lanka would be embroiled in a blood bath, yet God's Grace would be sufficient for us and would keep us safe in this period of virtual war.

* * *

April 6, 1971: Sirisena, a young man, who was born a Buddhist, had, on that day, visited Frank Williams, who had given him a copy of the Gospel of John. Carrying it in his pocket he had come to the heart of Colombo. When he was in the city the rumour spread that the insurgents were now attacking and had arrived in trucks and were assailing security personnel. Buses ground to a halt and the roads were a confusion of panic-stricken people desperately trying to get home before the insurgents arrived. He had noticed several bodies lying on the road as he rushed towards his home along Galle Road towards Nugegoda and on to his home in Kotte. Many were running along a stretch of that road.

As he had passed by Temple Trees, the residence of the Prime Minister, he and about ten other youth had been stopped by armed soldiers and asked to form a circle. They were all commanded to raise their hands and keep them raised. Soldiers trained their guns on these men as they were being questioned. When it came to Sirisena's turn, the officer asked him, "What is that in your pocket?"

"It is a Christian Gospel Portion," he answered and gave it the officer to have a closer look. He glanced through the first few pages and then told Sirisena to get out and run home. In his testimony he later said when the gun was aimed at him he was not sure whether he would be shot dead or not. At that moment, he began to pray and said he would become a Christian if God saved him from being killed. Right then and there standing before a soldier aiming his gun at him, he said a great peace came over him and when he had been asked to get out and run home, he knew it was the pure Grace of God that had protected him from certain death caused by this insurgent warfare!

Sirisena attended the Lanka Bible College, graduated, and went on to Pastor a Church. He has been in the Christian ministry now, for over 25 years, and has won many souls to Jesus Christ. He is working among non-Christians in the north of Colombo.

The curfew was fully in place until the end of May. It was gradually relaxed, although a State of Emergency was imposed and anyone could be arrested and taken into custody.

Rohana was arrested and imprisoned. Thousands of youth who were apprehended languished in jail while and an unknown number – some estimate it to be several thousands – were killed and buried. Some police stations were erecting tall barricades then, to protect their personnel. A Police Station sprang up next to the Temple Trees, with armed soldiers on guard, round the clock.

All meetings except the Sunday Service were discontinued and much prayer was made for the nation.

During this period in May, since we were unable to hold open air services or outreach work, I felt we must share the Gospel through Gospel Literature. I placed a small advertisement, costing one dollar at that time, in the newspaper, offering a free correspondence course based on the Bible. Within a few days, over 150 letters requesting the course arrived in our mailbox. Every day the numbers kept on increasing so much so that we had to convert one room at Lighthouse into an office. A pastor suggested a name for this ministry and it was called '*Jeevana Ganga*' or 'River of Life'. Brother Jayakrishna, one of the Elders, was appointed as Director and later Patrick Lazarus assisted him.

By 1999, over 5,000 people had been enrolled in the course and over two million pieces of Christian literature were sent out by post or distributed. Under the new director, Walter Jayarajah, the staff had increased to ten people who were handling the work.

Walter Jayarajah was raised in Jaffna. In 1971, Dr. Mjourd and I were conducting a crusade in the Jaffna YMCA and Walter was present. He came forward and was saved. He had an evocative voice and produced over twenty volumes of Tamil songs. He passed away some years ago and his wife Gnana is continuing the work under the name POLIMA.

Among those who were to work in *Jeevana Ganga* was a young lady who was a member of the now proscribed JVP[4] movement. Sheila was one of the hundreds of girls who joined the militant movement. She told us later that she had the word "motherland or death" engraved on her thigh before being accepted into the movement! Amazing Grace found this dissident and made her a disciple of Christ.

We were just cuddling our first-born son Mark, who was born in March 1972, when Stig Anthin came to the Hospital with another piece of good news: The Lighthouse Church had purchased the spacious house belonging to Mrs. Vanderstraten who was migrating to Australia. That move was another milestone in the work of God in Kandy. The LBI moved to Piachaud Gardens.

We needed more space and built two new classrooms adjoining the church building. We held regular Graduation services at Scott Hall since our church was not able to accommodate the visitors who came for the service. Among those who were invited to address the Graduation service were Dr. Tissa Weerasinghe and Rev. Don Rubesh.

By the end of 1989, LBI relocated from Piachaud Gardens to Christopher Road, Peradeniya. As the student enrolment began to increase the need for a larger, neutral campus was necessary. It was important for the image of the school, as well as for every day purposes. We were informed that the Hebron School building in Peradeniya was up for sale. It was a four acre property with several buildings including an auditorium, several large halls and classrooms, as well as a Principal's bungalow. Peradeniya was the home of the first University Campus. Its huge campus and architecturally striking buildings were widely admired. Peradeniya, too had a salubrious climate conducive for study and living. The property was owned by Mrs. David, the wife of the deceased principal.

By this time we had already located a bare land in Primrose Garden of around forty perches and had drawn up the blue print for the building. When we heard that Hebron was for sale we rushed to meet Mrs. David

---

[4] The JVP or the *Janathā Vimukthi Peramuna* (People's Liberation Front) is a Marxist-Leninist, communist political party in Sri Lanka. The party was involved in two armed uprisings against the ruling governments in 1971 (SLFP) and 1987-89 (UNP). After 1989, JVP entered into democratic politics by participating in the 1994 parliamentary general election.

in the Principal's bungalow. It was situated at the entrance of the property, with a slight ascent.

Hildegard and I talked with her regarding the sale price and she said that properties in that area were high in demand and so she could sell her property for around two million rupees. We politely asked her whether she would consider lowering her price, but, she was adamant.

I vividly remember rising up from my chair to show her we were leaving since the price she was asking for was far too high. In my mind I knew we had just Rs. 9,000 in the Hatton National Bank, which was needed for our operation. I felt God was able to change this to Rs. 900,000 – a bargain even at that time. I told her we would offer 9 lakhs[5] and calmly walked away from her verandah. Hildegard said later on, that she was quite surprised that I had made such a low offer. There are times when your faith must be initiated and activated by the Holy Spirit. This was one such moment. We had no idea how this amount of money could be raised.

We walked away from her bungalow and began to pray for God's provision for us to buy this campus built for a school. It had everything a school needed and ample land for expansion. She came to my office at LBI a few times to see whether we would agree to her already stated price but we told here we were unable to do so. One day she rushed to my office all frantic, panting and visibly shaken. She told us that Government, under President J. R. Jayawardene, had acquired the entire school for its Audit Department.

Shortly afterwards, we drove up to the school to find all the classrooms occupied by clerks and personnel of the audit department. This was a tough setback for us.

Some months later, we had two visitors from Sweden. They had asked us to come for dinner at the Queen's Hotel downtown and later, invited us to their room for coffee. Afterwards we suggested a time of prayer and the four of us prayed, albeit without any specific petition. In prayer, one of the brothers began to speak in tongues for a brief moment.

We bid our goodbyes and as we left the room, Hildegard was very excited and asked me if I thought the brother knew French, for, in his Prayer he had said, "'*L école ici déjà*' – 'the school is already standing.'" We

[5] A lakh is 100,000

turned back and got to know that he had no knowledge of French. The Spirit had used this language to let us know that the school was standing and there was no need to search elsewhere.

On our return home, I read a passage from the Bible which was from Isaiah which too spoke about joy and gladness emanating from this place. This was a *Rhema*[6] from the Lord to me. The Spirit spoke to Hildegard in French and to me in English. Neither of these languages were our mother tongue. How great are His wonders he performs for his people!

We then were assured that God would provide for us, even though all the circumstances were at odds. We were in waiting mode, fully trusting Him. The promises of God are realized by faith and patience.

Not too long after this, Mrs. David came to see us, and this time, she was bursting with happiness and excitement. "What is the news?" we asked her? She said, "The President has, by special decree, commanded the Audit Department to quit the school and hand it back to her."

Incredible! She showed us the letter written to her by the President informing her of his decision. We, of course, were thoroughly excited and decided to do our best to raise the money. Mrs. David now agreed to sell the property for the price we offered. She probably was glad to sell it before someone persuaded the President to change his mind!

* * *

Stig Anthin, just two years after his arrival in Sri Lanka, had to leave back to Sweden as there was a visa problem and he was constantly ill, the doctors unable to diagnose his sickness. Around this time, Don Allen and his family came to Sri Lanka and were staying in Nuwara-Eliya. As they were unhappy with the spicy food and the cold climate, we invited them to come and stay with us in Kandy. We lived along Peradeniya Road at that time. We had ample room for them and Don would bring a generous supply of vegetables and groceries to help our budget.

He taught at LBI and was an amiable person. It was always a pleasure to be around him. Not being able to stay longer, Don too had left back to the

---

[6] Rhema (in Greek) means an utterance or spoken word. It's usage in Christian Theology Rhema is the revealed word of God, as an utterance from God to the heart of the reader through the Holy Spirit.

USA after just a few months.

I wrote to Don and told him that the Hebron school was again for sale and also the amount we needed. Don had stood on those very grounds and prayed that we would one day occupy it.

He was very impressed with the LBI and on his return to the US, invited me to be one of the Speakers at a Renewal Conference in Dallas, sponsored by the Tyler Street Methodist Church. After the conference, he took me to visit the Christ for the Nations campus which had about 1,000 students. I was to meet Mrs. Gordon Lindsay, whose husband was the founder of CFNI.

At this meeting, which was a mid-week staff prayer meeting, I shared how we were saved at a Brethren Church and how we had began to pray for revival. I told them how I had been inspired, reading books written by Lindsay. There was one book which kept stirring my heart, *"Bible Days are Here Again"*. I then told her how we were baptized in the Holy Spirit in a Brethren church and went on to hold large mass healing campaigns which were previously unheard of in our Buddhist nation. When I finished she told someone to bring a tape-recorder and record what I had just said to the group earlier. I willingly obliged.

The next month I received a copy of the CFNI magazine and across its centre page was this headline: *"Five Buildings at a Bargain Price."* It contained pictures of the bungalow, the auditorium and a few others. There was a picture of me preaching at the Negombo mass crusade. I then realized that the article in the magazine contained my testimony and the inspiration I had received by reading the books written by Gordan Lindsay. Needless to say readers were confident that they were investing in a worthy cause in a needy land.

Readers of the magazine responded generously and the funds to buy the building were remitted to the Hatton National Bank. It was a great day when Hildegard, Krishnarajah and I sat in front of the desk of the Bank Manager and signed the deeds. We gave Mrs. David the cheque and she gave me a key ring holding the keys for the premises. Amidst a few other rusty ones, was the main key – a long, black iron key which reminded me of the type used to open dungeon doors. When I received that key, I knew this was symbolic of numerous doors that we would open to proclaim the

Gospel and plant new churches in this nation. The building was now ours at last! Whatever cost that was needed for interior repairs and changes was met by the school.

Some months prior to the purchase of the property, I had been accepted as a candidate for the M. A. Degree by the Fuller Theological Seminary in Pasadena, California. Now Ranjit was then appointed Principal of the LBI and, in November of 1979, I left for the USA with my family, which by then had grown to include three sons, Mark, Stephan and Dennis. We arrived at the Los Angeles Airport to reside in Pasadena, on the very same day that Ranjit flew back to Sri Lanka.

13

Ranjit Appointed Principal of the LBC. The First Sri Lankan Martyr. Terry Jones, Jim Yarbrough and the Prayer Tower. The Significant Growth of the LBC. Pastor Jacob Ratnam, Ministry Among the Youth and Winner's Camp. Fire Falls at Winner's Camp

THE LBI WAS RE-NAMED THE LANKA BIBLE COLLEGE; THE NEW address was Christopher Road, Peradeniya and the new principal – Ranjit De Silva. A new epoch for the school had begun. The BFC story repeated again!

Ranjit had come back with a M. A. Degree from the Fuller Theological Seminary. He was a scholar and an excellent organizer. He saw talent and potential in people and recruited them to his troops. On his watch, the school became a truly inter-denominational institution. A member of the Faculty was an Anglican Minister loaned to the School by the then Bishop of Colombo. The staff was made up of members of other churches in Kandy.

As our vision was to upgrade and accredit the school, we had sent promising students out, to get their degrees. Among them were Danny Moses and Maxi Abraham. They too returned at this time to lecture at the LBC.

The Library expanded and Sinhala and Tamil translations of English books were now undertaken. A new two-storeyed building to house students and staff was built and the Cafeteria was enlarged to accommodate 100 students for meals. Discipline, order and a beautiful and well-maintained campus was now emerging. The LBC was accredited by the ATA (Asia Theological Association).

On Ranjit's watch, one of the students that graduated was Lionel Jayasinghe. He had come from Hambantota, the deep south of the island. He went back to his home and pioneered a church in the heart of the Buddhist homeland.

During the second JVP insurrection, some men had called on Lionel in the dead of the night and demanded that he come out and speak to them. As Lionel had approached the men, one of them had fired a shot and Lionel had fallen to the ground, bleeding profusely. He had died before his wounds could be treated as no hospital was open at that time of night because of curfews imposed, and no one would have dared to leave their houses at night. The JVP now had a strong following in the south and were bent on spreading anarchy and bedlam wherever they could. It was a night of terror and bloodshed for the Jayasinghe family. He was the first modern martyr of the Sri Lankan Church. After the funeral, his wife Nalini managed to gather the shocked and scattered people. The church slowly began to re-assemble and grow.

When I was interviewing prospective students, I met a young man who told us that he was from Nalini's church in Hambantota. I asked him if he wasn't afraid to go and evangelize to the people of that area to which he replied, "I know the Power of the Gospel and if need be, I am prepared to die like Pastor Lionel!"

Lionel's red blood was shed and drenched the earth. The JVP thought that by removing him the church would eventually fold up and his wife and relatives would leave town. But the miracle of Grace in times of War again triumphed over brutality, and the light of the Gospel broke through utter darkness, and is now turning potential insurgents into missionaries.

* * *

Don Allen and Terry Jones were former ordained Methodist Missionaries whose passion for souls brought them to Sri Lanka. Terry arrived first in Sri Lanka, in 1976. He was a graduate of the Asbury Seminary in Kentucky and was a student during an extraordinary outpouring of the Holy Spirit upon that seminary. Terry had another friend whom I had met in 1974, in Dallas.

Terry had a vision: to build a Prayer Tower on the LBC campus. He produced this picture on a Bulletin and had it widely circulated among his friends for prayer. While he was struggling to raise money for the Prayer Tower, Jim Yarbrough's son Paul died in a tragic car accident. The motorist who caused the collision was charged and had to pay a substantial sum as compensation. When Jim heard that Terry was struggling to raise funds for this project, he called Terry, informing him that he would pay for the building with the compensation received due to the death of his son.

While grieving with Jim and his wife, Terry appraised him about the cost of the building. Jim, still broken-hearted, sent a substantial amount of money to pay for the tower. Today there stands in the midst of the LBC campus, a striking building dedicated for prayer.

As I meditated on this loss and gift, I was reminded of what the Bible said of Abel, "being dead yet speaketh". Paul is dead and with the Lord. Yet he is speaking through all who come to pray to God at the Prayer Tower. The Prayer Tower stands as a memorial to Paul Yarbrough.

Ranjit left and re-joined the Fuller Seminary as a candidate for his Ph.D. programme. Enar Stahre took on the role of Principal and served until his departure to Sweden. He was instrumental in raising support from churches in Sweden interested in the LBC.

With the departure of Stahre, Ben Manikam was appointed the next Principal. Ben was with Campus Crusade, a good-looking young man, prepared to take the school to the next level. The enrolment began to increase significantly. A class which had eight students was now bursting with forty. Ben used his organizational and public relations skills to bring in manpower and financial resources from Switzerland and other nations to construct several of the much needed buildings. The stretch of land between the Principal's bungalow and the school belonged to the relatives of Mrs. David. That piece of property was purchased for Rs. 15 million thus preventing any "unwanted" construction. Under Ben's watch, the Graduate Centre for Studies was built in Colombo providing diploma and degree courses to students. This Centre is a boon to Pastors, Workers and Laymen who are unable to go Residential. LBC held its Graduation Ceremony at the BMICH, one of the largest conference halls in Colombo which was attended by a large responsive assemblage.

The Lanka Bible College & Seminary has grown in leaps and

bounds with over 600 of the most promising leaders representing all denominations enrolled in Undergraduate and Graduate level study. LBCS programs remain the most sought after by the church in Sri Lanka. Rev. Lal Senanayake is the present Principal of the College. His efforts have brought in many International scholars to teach at the LBC. Rev. Ben Manikam currently serves as the Director of LBC Graduate studies in Colombo. Many a leader has lauded the LBC's impact on the Christian work and its growth in Sri Lanka. Here are what a few have had to say:

"Never afraid to try new and innovative methods, LBCS has consistently taken up the challenges of the church and the nation."

Godfrey Yogarajah
General Secretary, NCEASL
General Secretary, Evangelical Fellowship Asia International Leadership Team, World Evangelical Alliance

"LBCS has hit on a formula that will surely yield rich dividends for years to come."

Ajith Fernando
National Director, Youth for Christ Sri Lanka

"LBCS has come to the forefront as an educational institute that provides the required curriculum and training."

Eraj Wijesinghe
Chairman, Colombo Stock Exchange,
Chairman, Bartleet Group

"LBCS is in the forefront of leadership training and institutional development in Sri Lanka. I am impressed by the high quality of research produced by students."

Rt. Rev. Narendra John
Secretary for Accreditation & Educational Development, Asia Theological Assoc.
Bishop, Free Methodist Church

"OCA has identified LBCS as the most important institution in Sri Lanka for Building the Church and the nation."

Rev. Stuart Brooking
Executive Director, Overseas Council, Australia

"LBCS continues to be at the cutting edge of addressing complex issues faced by the church."

Pastor Adrian De Visser
International Deputy Director, Lausanne Committee for World Evangelization
Vice President for Partnership Development, Asian Access
Senior Pastor, Kithu Sevena

"LBC is indeed one of the premier leadership programmes in Asia."
Dr. Manfred Khol
Vice President of International Development, Overseas Council International

"The training at LBC has proved to work in Sri Lanka."
James Kanaganayagam
Managing Director, Back to the Bible, Sri Lanka

"LBC will have a lasting impact on the whole Sri Lankan Church for generations to come."
Rt. Rev. Dr. Hwa Yung
Bishop, Methodist Church in Malaysia

Pastor Jacob Ratnam was one of the graduates of the Lanka Bible College. After his graduation, he established a Church in Gampola, a neighbouring town to Kandy. He is devoted to saving youth and bringing them into a deeper walk with the Lord. To achieve this goal, he organized the Winner's Camp which has to date, been held for 25 consecutive years. These camps are held during the April or August holidays. Most of those who attend are between the ages of fourteen and twenty-one and come from churches from across the island. Barring just two camps, I have been a guest speaker at this Camp for 23 years.

My theme has always been the Baptism of the Holy Spirit and Endowment of Power for service. I present a short message on the passages, about being filled with the Holy Spirit, and then pray for many youth at the camp. Whenever the altar call is given, the altars are crammed with young people, both boys and girls, eager to receive the Gift of the Father.

Hundreds of young people have not only spoken in tongues at the altars but they have also received visions and been impressed to enter fulltime ministry. When they returned to their churches, they have, by their testimony and witness, galvanized others in the church. At these altar calls, we have felt the tangible presence of God in these services. Needless to say, I have prayed for a countless number of people to be baptized in the Holy Spirit, both here and abroad, and have seen them jubilant as they spoke in new tongues.

At these meetings, I have been often reminded of the corral at Bethesda, for which we are always thankful, but we are also glad we left the corral and are now galloping to all the nations of the Earth.

14

The Lighthouse Church. Establishing Churches. The Red and Pale Horsemen on the March. Threat from the JVP. Our Years at Lighthouse Church. Team Arrested by Panwila Police.

LIGHTHOUSE CHURCH HAD ITS BEGINNINGS WITH SISTER HUTCHINS was a prayer group and Sunday School at Mulgampola, and then moved to 502 Peradeniya Road, Kandy. I first visited LHC in 1963 for the Revival meetings conducted by the Swedish Brethren.

Rev. P. Krishnarajah writes in the 40th Anniversary Commemorative Issue in 2003 about the inception of the LHC:

> On the 12th day of May 1963, the Lighthouse Church was formed and set in order after much prayer. Rev. Tage Sjoberg prayed over the small congregation and asked the Lord to bless and increase the flock. The Lord had been faithful during the past forty years and He kept to His word. "The one who calls you is faithful and He will do it." *(I Thessalonians 5:24).*
>
> The little flock of 12 members in 1963, had multiplied to 4,229 by the grace of God who gave the increase. The Lighthouse Church was planted like a small mustard seed, which grew to be a big tree with several branches. Today there are 16 churches and 49 house churches.
>
> Sister Hutchins, who was sent by the Lighthouse Mission in England, had been working faithfully for many years. People used to gather in a small rented house at Mulgampola, as an effective prayer group and a good Sunday school conducted in English. In 1958, they moved to a large house with a spatial garden at 502, Peradeniya Road. In 1959, Rev. Enar Stahre was invited to help the work by Sister Hutchins.

In the early seventies, the church opened its facilities to the Lanka Bible Institute, headed by Pastor V. Chandy. Simultaneously, the church started growing with the planting of extension churches around Kandy. Some of the workers, trained at the Lanka Bible Institute, were able to pioneer in the extension churches.

Emmanuel Jayakrishna became the pastor in 1978 and, with the addition of Alexi Liyanage and S. Nithiyanandan as Assistant Pastors, there was a rapid growth in both the Sinhala and Tamil congregations.

During the latter part of 1984, Dr. V. Chandy was appointed as Pastor and Emmanuel Jayakrishna became the Associate Pastor. The Pastoral team during this period worked fervently with several crusades in several areas under the leadership of Pastor Chandy. More extension churches were established during this period. Substantial funds were raised to help build new extension churches.

During this period, the Sinhala and Tamil departments started functioning under their respective pastors. At present, they function under Pastor Rienzie de Silva and Pastor S. Nithiyanandan respectively, with several assistants.

P. Krishnarajah
Senior Pastor

I spent almost thirty years in Kandy, nearly nine years as Principal of LBI and then eighteen years as Senior Pastor of the LHC. The editorial and my commentary give a brief glimpse of the progression and advance of the LHC. These twenty and seven years, these 700 plus months have seen us facing two of the most fierce and most ferocious groups to ever torment this island nation.

The JVP, or Che Guevara squads, re-emerged with greater vengeance than during the April Insurgency. Rohana Wijeweera was released from jail and unleashed 42 months of distress on the country. The Army and Police were powerless to meet the onslaught of these rampaging hordes of savages. Their *modus operandi* was to issue a "Hartal" leaflet, ordering all shops and even hospitals to close down on any given day. The penalty for defying the edict would be death. They carried out countless executions of innocent people who went against their order. The Red Horseman of the Apocalypse was now galloping through the land. *(Rev 6:3-4).*

The colour red represents a sword ready to spill blood. Civil war had broken out; the JVP were hell-bent to create anarchy and to capture power. The JVP killed a bus driver in Kandy, who disobeyed their order not to drive on that day. A baker was killed as he sold a loaf of bread in the morning at Bowala. Young men would now play cricket on the once busy Peradeniya Road on Hartal day. The aim of the JVP was to create mayhem and panic in the country, and then take over.

A doctor living next to our house at Piachaud Garden was standing outside his house on the day of the Hartal. He told us if he went to the hospital he would be shot dead. On the previous day he ordered that all pregnant mothers be sent home as there would be no doctors on duty that day. It brings to mind the Scripture where Jesus speaks of the times of the end: "But woe to those who are pregnant and to those who are nursing babies in those days! For there will be great distress in the land and wrath upon his people." *(Luke 21:23)*

By evening most homes were shrouded in darkness. Lights went out as early as seven in the evening. The JVP went into schools and coerced them to participate in the rebellion. One day we heard that there was a commotion on Peradeniya Road and drove by to see what was happening. As we came close to a girl's school we realized the road was defended by a large party of policeman who were looking up at a hillock, on which a group of girls were standing. They must have been between twelve and fourteen years old. The principal had suspected the possible outbreak of a riot and had called the police. These girls stood behind the safety of the barbed wire fence and called out in loud voices at the uniformed constables, "Hey! Police dogs! Get out of here!" all the while making rude gestures at them.

What amazed us is that the policeman, armed with machine guns, looked on calmly at these misguided girls. Shocked at such behaviour, we returned to the safety of our home on Piachaud Gardens. The system of education had taken a tail-spin and never regained control of itself. The audacity of these skinny girls to challenge the police force was a signal that something has seriously gone wrong with schools and their values. The unemployed Sinhala youth were now on the verge of grabbing power from the Government.

In 1989, mid-way through the "tribulation", a letter was delivered to the

Lighthouse Church office. Alexi Liyanage brought the letter to our house situated close to the Church. The moment I saw the envelope, something told me that there was a perilous message inside it.

There was an earlier order sent out by the JVP to close up all shops and establishments in Kandy for two days – Saturday and Sunday. Almost every shop pulled down its shutters and by the afternoon, the streets were empty. We closed our office and all who remained were sent home. On Sunday we had our services as usual with a low attendance and some apprehension as to what would happen if he JVP squads saw us at church.

This letter, typed in Sinhala, warned us that since we did not obey their order to close the church on those two days they were giving us another warning. 'You will close the church for two weeks and if not you will see the end of barrel of an AK-47. This is your final warning.' There was no address given.

We summoned all the elders and pastors and prayed fervently. Then Alexi suggested that we go and meet an acquaintance of his to ensure that this was a JVP letter not someone else's. With the letter in my pocket I drove Alexi to a village and down a road to a small house. This was the home of a *Vedamahathaya*[1]. We went inside the rather dark room and the smell of crushed herbs and *gingelly*[2] oil permeated the room. An elderly man, dressed in a sarong came forward. He recognized Alexi. I returned to my car where I sat there, waiting in silence. A short while later, Alexi came out of the house, visibly disturbed. He got into the car and said, "Let's go from here."

Whether the doctor had some connection with the movement was not certain. Alexi explained that directives from the JVP have a certain code within it. That code was to print one letter of the alphabet upside down! He showed me how that one letter was typed upside down to indicate that it was original and not a fake.

We informed all our believers that we would not hold services for the next two Sundays; however we would be holding meetings in 10 different households each Sunday. There were voices lifted up against it, saying we should not be afraid of anybody but meet as usual on Sunday. We had to

---

[1] A doctor of Ayurvedic (or indigenous herbal) medicine

[2] An edible vegetable oil derived from sesame seeds, also known as sesame oil

explain to them that since this is a church and we have a large congregation including women and children, we could not take responsibility for their lives in case anything went wrong.

For the first time, people realized the luxury of the freedom to go to church on a Sunday and worship the Lord. The Sundays that followed the ban, saw the church full! The Red Horseman was now riding in full supremacy. This perilous period saw the whole church on its knees, praying and fasting for protection from the Insurgents who were hiding in safe-houses in the Kandy District.

* * *

Our years at Lighthouse Church were divided into two parts. First I was part of the ministry from 1970-1979, when I was Principal of the LBI. The second part was from 1984-1998 when I was the Senior Pastor.

During the first years, we were involved in the huge mass crusades that drew in thousands of people. Details of this will be in ensuing chapters. The second period began when I was appointed pastor of the church with Emmanuel as Associate Pastor. In these years we saw expansion of the church in Kandy and in the Central Province.

The English congregation grew rapidly and Hildegard started the women's ministry which was not heard of at that time. She started with just two people, but sheer persistence saw the group grow to a lively clique of eager women who met every Wednesday in the church or at our home. Even women not belonging to our church started coming. Hildegard always had a heart of compassion and she won their confidence and love. They felt free to share their burdens and dreams for their families and children. They were soon involved in interesting bible studies and intercessory prayer.

More and more women understood the role they played in their family and soon they sent their children to school, blessing them and believing for the salvation of their husbands. Many prayers were answered and we are glad to say the women's ministry is still ongoing in the Lighthouse Church.

Hildegard was always thrilled to hear when any members who moved to other countries wrote to tell us that they were now leaders in women's groups in their churches.

During the JVP years, the Sinhala congregation saw a rapid increase in the number of people attending the services led by Alexi Liyanage. The Tamil congregation had seen a burst of growth since Nithiyanandan took over its leadership and today, the Sunday Service has around 400-500 people.

Nithiyanandan himself was born into a Hindu family and his father was the President of the Temple in Panwila. The story of Nithyandan's conversion began with Ariyam, a graduate of the LBI who began to work in Panwila. He invited Nithiyanandan to come and visit him. During the conversation Nithiyanandan was angry that new religions were being brought to traditional Hindu areas. After a somewhat heated argument, Nithiyanandan agreed to pray with Ariyam. During the prayer something implausible happened. A Spirit of conviction came upon Nithi and he began to weep. When he rose from prayer he was re-born and a believer in Christ.

He returned to his house and told his family that he had become a Christian. Immediately, his father ordered him out of the house and poured water from a bowl to the floor symbolizing that his son had died. For nine long years he was forbidden to come back to the house. This was the price paid for believing in Christ as Lord and Saviour.

New churches were planted in Matale, Galboda, Nawalapitiya, Galaha, Rajawela, Kegalle, Mawattegama and Madulkella, to mention some of them. The stories of how these churches were built, the opposition that we encountered, the sacrifices paid by the pastors and their families, the miracle of divine provision would fill the pages of another book. We have no space to record these narratives.

I had the prayers and support of the Elders then serving the church and the faithful, loyal and loving support of the members. Suffice to say that in 1963, there were twelve members and by 2003 the total membership was over 4,000, with nearly fifty branch churches and 45 ordained and licensed ministers. To God be the glory. The Elders were Moses, Stahre, Emmanuel, Krishnarajah, and Reinzie de Silva.

Tuwan Bongso served as my Administrator for fifteen years. He was a former DIG (Deputy Inspector General of Police), a tall, dignified figure with flawless English and a courteous manner. He was born into a Muslim family and experienced a marvellous conversion. He was widely respected and known to the police authorities and was able to help us resolve many issues that arose during the uprising of both the JVP and the LTTE.

During these years, there was open opposition to church work, especially in Kandy and in other villages. The police knew Mr. Bongso was in our church and complaints and false accusations against us were dismissed by the Kandy Central Range Police department, because of the immense respect they had for him.

Hildegard was supported by the congregation and the Ladies Group all throughout those years. At the height of the Indian food dropping[3] there was tension even among some Christians who were sympathetic to one side or the other. Much tension was diffused when people realized that neither my wife nor I was ethnically a Sinhala or a Tamil. We were able to bring much needed peace between all quarters at this critical time.

The church today has appointed P. Krishnarajah as its senior Pastor. Krishnarajah was a senior staff officer at the Agriculture Department and held a Masters Degree from Canada. He is an able administrator and preacher. He served on the LBI board when I was heading it and during my entire tenure at LHC, was on our board, and his advice and counsel was indispensable. He is still the Chairman of the LBC board; probably the longest standing board member of any Christian Organization.

This chapter on the LHC Church would not be complete without narrating an incident that took place during the first JVP insurrection. The LBI and LHC brothers and sisters went to the Knuckles Range estate to conduct a Medical Clinic headed by Dr. Nagendran. In the evening, they had returned to Kandy with a few brothers, having finished the clinic. Nagendran drove with Anthin who had a yellow Volkswagen car. They had taken a consignment of tracts for free distribution. When they were turning down the road from Madulkalle to Kandy, a policeman had signalled them to stop. The constable was alone and wanted to hitch a ride to the Panwila Police Station. They readily consented and he climbed

[3] A mission undertaken by the Indian Air Force to air-drop supplies over the besieged town of Jaffna in Sri Lanka on 4 June 1987 in support of LTTE during the Sri Lankan Civil War.

into the rear seat. As they travelled along the winding, hilly road, the policeman had noticed a heap of tracts lying on the seat written in Tamil and Sinhala. He picked up a Sinhala tract and began reading. This was a tract telling the story of the Philippine soldiers who hid in the jungle during World War and kept on living inside the forest not knowing that the war was finished. There was a picture of some soldiers living in the jungle wearing army uniforms.

The policeman, suspecting them to be part of the insurgency, surreptitiously called the Panwila Police and told them that insurgents were driving towards them in a yellow Volkswagen. As the party rounded the bend near the police station, a posse of policeman armed with machine guns pulled them over and held a gun to their heads. They were hauled into the Station and interrogated for hours after first being put into a cell. Not being allowed to phone or contact anyone, they were soon pulled out, questioned and harassed for over three gruesome hours. At the end of their ordeal, they were finally released.

We had already returned to the church in Kandy and were waiting for Anthin and Nagendran. Deeply worried about their delay, we had started praying earnestly for their safety.

At around ten that night we saw Anthin drive up to the church and park under the porch. His face was ashen and pale. Nagendran related the story of what had happened. They were released since the HQI at the Kandy Police, was a colleague of Nagendran at Trinity College. What a sigh of relief we breathed, and we thanked the Lord for this deliverance. All explanation given to the Panwila Police was not accepted until the call came from the HQI to release them.

We were incensed and furious that innocent people, especially a foreigner, were arrested and detained in a remand room for so long a time. A few days later, when tempers had cooled off, we decided to go back to the Police Station and give all of them a free New Testament, well-wrapped and wishing them God's blessings.

We took about fifteen copies and went back to the Panwila Police station sans Anthin. When we walked in, they recognized Nagendran and looked suitably embarrassed. We explained to them who we were and why we went to Knuckles estate. They took the copies with some mixed feelings. I then asked the Sub Inspector of Police whether we could hold an open air meeting in the streets. They were now somewhat troubled and puzzled at our boldness to return to the place of arrest. We stood in the street in front of the Police Station and began to sing and preach. A crowd soon gathered, who knew of the arrest of the white man in the Volkswagen car. A number raised their hands for the altar call, all the while carefully watched by policemen from their windows. At the altar call we took down the names of people who wanted to accept Christ, and later, Brother Jayakrishna started regular Sunday services. Today, in the heart of Panwila Town, there is a church building that can hold nearly 500 people!

Years later we met a young man called Anthony who had now became a member of the church. He told Nagendran that when they were arrested he was an onlooker and had seen a man dressed in dazzling white near them. He was then a Hindu. He said he can never forget the image of that man in white and he now believes that was an angel sent to protect them.

Praise the Lord! In the midst of the raging insurgency arrest, remand, and police interrogation God's Grace was abundantly present. Marvellous Grace; Wonderful Grace that changed a seeming holdup into a fruitful triumph for Gods' people.

15

The Liberation Tamil Tigers. The H-Bomb. The Central Bank Bombing: 10.15 am, Jan. 31, 1996. A Miraculous Escape. The Pale Horseman of the Apocalypse Rides into the Heart of the City.

Before I describe the Central Bank Bombing, it is important to comprehend the basic nature of the Tamil Tigers and the reason for their formation. The LTTE was a separatist militant movement that believed in violence and anarchy to achieve a homeland for the Tamil speaking people of the North and East. With the introduction of the Sinhala Only Act, and selection of students to university based on ethnicity by the Sirimavo Bandaranaike regime, the Tamils felt that they had been marginalized by the Sinhalese. The riots of '58, '77 and '83 were the immediate motivation for the rise of the militant Tamil Tigers.

The LTTE was founded in 1977 by Velupillai Prabakaran, whose avowed aim was to achieve an independent Tamil homeland. They were the first to create the H-Bomb (Human Bomb). Bombs were strapped to the bodies of willing young Tamil Tigers to blow up army camps, electrical installations and public buildings. They were the only Terrorist organization in the world to assassinate two world leaders: the Prime Minister of India and the President of Sri Lanka.[1]

The Tamil Tigers had different uniforms or fatigues for their cadres.

[1] Rohan Gunaratna, "*The Rebellion in Sri Lanka: Sparrow Tactics to Guerrilla Warfare (1971–1996)*"

Those involved in normal combat were given uniforms with tiger stripes. Sea Tigers wore blue and the suicide corps wore black. Female soldiers would have their hair braided and not worn long as long hair would be unsafe in a battle. Most of them were young and from low castes. Weapons were sacred and if any combatants lost one, it would not be replaced. All Tigers were given a *kuppi*[2] to bite into in case they were captured. Hundreds died by swallowing this poison.

Symbolically, the LTTE were the forerunners of the dreaded fourth horseman of the Apocalypse; the Pale Horse: "When He opened the fourth seal, I heard the voice of the fourth living creature saying, "Come and see." So I looked, and behold, a pale horse. And the name of him who sat on it was Death, and Hades followed with him. And power was given to them over a fourth of the earth, to kill with sword, with hunger, with death, and by the beasts of the earth. *(Rev. 6:7-8)*

The Pale horse had a yellow or pallid colour. Some believe it is the colour of a corpse. This pale horse swept through the length and breadth of this island, leaving behind a stream of blood, devastation, ruin and death, unprecedented in the history of this nation. It is reported that 150,000 civilians and 15,000 Tiger cadres perished in the war, although this does not take into account soldiers who were killed in a battle which continued for nearly thirty years.

No one could stop the Pale Horseman as he rode in ferocity across this nation and in many ways and forms, had rejected the Prince of Peace. The LTTE war that began in 1983, only ended in 2009, when the Sri Lankan Army defeated and killed Prabakaran.

* * *

On the 31st of January, 1996, Hildegard and I had to come down from Kandy to the Customs Department to clear baggage that had come from Germany. Usually we would leave Kandy early to be in Colombo when the offices opened. We filled the forms at the Customs and proceeded to the Times building where we had to collect additional documentation. The four storey Times building is one of the oldest buildings in the Fort. Close by stands the Central Bank of Ceylon, a modern building built by a

[2] *Kuppi* – Cyanide Capsule

German construction company and completed in 1964.

The Central Bank is on Janadhipathi Mawatha, formerly known as Queen's Street. The next street on the right is Chatham Street with many jewellery stores. To get to the Times building you had go down Chatham Street, cross York Street and enter the Times Building through Bristol Street on the left.

The Central Bank building is in the heart of the commercial centre of the island. The Ceylinco building, one of the tallest, stands across the Central Bank.

We drove down to Colombo with our driver, Nimal. At around 9.45 that morning, we passed my old work place, the Central Bank, and turned on to Chatham Street. Parking the van, we told our driver to wait for us till we returned from the Customs.

We took the elevator to the fourth floor of the Times building and at the office we met a friend of mine whom I knew from my students days. He was very cordial and accepted our documents for approval. We were seated in front of him, discussing matters, while a clerk was busy attending to our papers. It was 10:15. Out of nowhere came a sudden, ear-splitting blast that shook the entire building and we felt the aftershocks of the explosion on the fourth floor. Parts of the ceiling came down around us. I saw the vase on the table flung to the floor. Hildegard felt sick in her stomach saying afterwards that it felt as if someone had punched her. We knew it was the blast of a bomb, but where had it exploded?

Everyone was peering through the windows down at the streets below, trying to figure out where the bomb had exploded. Hundreds of crows perched on trees took off at the sound off the explosion and their shrill croaks filled the air. It was then that we saw the plumes of smoke flooding out of different windows of the central bank. The smoke soon gave way to flames that began to flare up from out of the windows of every floor. The flames were leaping out of the building and the entire area was brimming with smoke.

We rushed downstairs and out onto the street. We had crossed York Street and were trying to make our way back to Queens Street, down Chatham. Hundreds upon hundreds of people were running, panicked; some bleeding, some soaked in blood.

I saw men running in panic; dazed and horrified. Their shirts looked like they were dyed red. We glanced up at the Bank of Ceylon building. The windows were shattered and almost all the other windows of adjacent buildings were smashed to pieces.

We crossed York Street against a tide of people trying to get away as fast as they could. We managed to push through to the Clock Tower which stands facing the Central Bank. There I saw a scene I will never forget. Smoke was pouring out of the windows of the bank as if a bowser was pumping water into an overhead tank. I stood still and thought, 'Am I in some Hollywood movie about World War II?'

The ground was covered with debris from the explosion. The truck which had carried the 400 pounds of explosives on its suicide mission was wrecked and shattered, pieces strewn everywhere. There was a huge crater where the bomb had detonated and the huge pillars of the bank were fractured and bent. The mangled bodies of the suicide bombers were scattered over the road. The blast had torn into the building and the basement had begun to flood.

People escaped through the staircase facing the sea. Ambulances were rushing on to the scene with their sirens blaring. Some men were carrying bodies away that were soaked in blood. The victims' clothes had been ripped off for the force of the blast. Some eight other adjacent buildings were damaged.

Ninety-one people were killed that day with over 400 injured. Around one hundred lost their sight. Among those who died were Sinhalese, Tamils, Burghers and eight foreigners.

We headed to where our van was parked, desperate to get away from the scene of such terror and head for the Every Home Crusade office where we were staying the night. We found Nimal who looked ashen and terrified. He had been requisitioned by the Police to take the injured to the General Hospital. He described the gruesome scene of bodies that were crushed by the blast and the floor of the ambulance covered with blood.

He had managed to return to the car park and we drove as fast as we could to Park Road where the EHC office was situated. There was a massive traffic block. All offices had closed early and people were in a rush to get home. The streets were jammed with vehicles, all heading away from the Fort area.

When we finally arrived and walked into the home of Dr. Sam Thevabalasingham, the founder and Director of Every Home Crusade. For over 40 years EHC Teams have visited millions of homes to leave a tract behind. Needless to say, he was certainly glad to see us back and alive. He knew we had gone to Fort that morning and he had heard the sound of the blast all the way to his home, a distance of about ten miles as the crow flies.

We told him that we had driven down the road in front of the Central Bank just thirty minutes before the bomb was detonated by the LTTE suicide bombers! Had we delayed, our van would have been caught up in the middle of the detonation and reduced to cinders. We stood together and gave thanks for the unbelievable protection God had provided for us that morning. Thirty minutes made the difference between life and death. Here was the overwhelming Grace of God in the middle of a fierce Terrorist War!

The Fourth Horseman of the Apocalypse had ridden his horse right through the heart of the City Centre. He left behind death, destruction, mutilated bodies and a thousand family members weeping for their loved ones whose only mistake had been to be inside or in the vicinity of the Central Bank as the Pale Horseman rode by.

The Bible predicts that in the last days, perilous times shall come and there shall be wars, rumours of war and earthquakes; men's hearts failing for fear of dreadful things that will happen before the return of Jesus Christ back to the earth. God has given men sufficient chances to repent and turn to Him but they have snubbed Him and the day of Grace is running out soon.

16

Mass Crusades. Miracles at People's Park. Argimiro Airborne. The Jaffna Crusade and its Fallout. The Healed Testify.

Back in February 1971 in Colombo, at People's Park, near the Zoological Gardens in Dehiwela, Frank Williams organized a Healing Crusade for Morris Cerrulo from America; a global evangelist with a powerful healing ministry. Cerrulo's associate was Argimiro Da Silva, an Argentinean-born Evangelist. The Prayer and Preparation meeting was held at Saraswathy Hall, Bambalapitiya. Over 500 were present and after prayer, Argimiro gave instructions on how to test the deaf, dumb and the blind when they were healed. I had not before seen a deaf or dumb person getting healed after prayer and doubted that this would actually happen.

I drove from Kandy and arrived at the Park to about 5,000 people gathered in front of the long stage. Floodlights lit up the park, and the singing could be heard a mile away. I was invited to come to the platform and take a seat with about twenty other pastors who were already seated. There were microphones set up, one for the speaker and the other two for the interpreters. Gladstone Abeysinghe, a veteran interpreter from the CPM was the Sinhala Interpreter.

I scanned the crowd and saw Don Rubesh standing there with a few others at the edge of the crowd. Knowing how disbelieving he was, I was surprised to see him at the first mass healing crusade. I found myself wondering what he really thought of the turnout that evening.

Argimiro was a powerful preacher. He emphasized that Jesus Christ is the same yesterday, today and forever. Then he signalled for us all to stand and pray with him. Everyone on the platform began to pray along with him, out loud and with lifted hands. I was still not convinced but joined in prayer since any failure to cure people with prayer would have been very embarrassing to all of us.

At the end of the prayer, he made a circular motion to the ushers and counsellors who were watching him, to turn around and look at the crowd. They did as they were told and he instructed them to observe the masses and look out for any sort of commotion and to go out to where these things took place, as there may be a person who had been healed.

Suddenly, we witnessed several outbreaks amongst the crowds in several parts of the ground.

There were two long ramps connected to the main platform, the one on the left for people to come up and testify and the other on the right for them to exit the platform and return to the grounds. I was standing close to the left ramp and saw people crowding around it and pushing their way to reach the speaker. Some managed to make their way to the edge of the platform. I saw an elderly man in white sarong and shirt trying to overtake the others. Seeing he was in a hurry to get to the Preacher for prayer, I asked him, "What is your problem?"

He replied, *"Gediyak,"* which meant a growth of some sort.

"Where is it?" I asked.

"It's gone!"

I was stunned. This was real. People were being healed, even on the first day. Many more came to the podium and began to give their testimony while the ushers were still testing people in the crowd. The deaf were tested by clapping while standing behind them. They would show the number of claps with raised fingers. The dumb began to speak recognizable words and those who were blind began to reach out and touch the nose or ears of the person testing them.

This was too much to take in for one day. I was absolutely overwhelmed at the amazing response of the people and the exhilarating atmosphere in the Park.

I left for Kandy, since our first child was due any day. Later, I heard that Morris Cerullo himself had arrived and preached on the last day with similar results. The crowd had now swelled to over 10,000.

Several months later, I met a journalist, Cecil Wickramanayake, who was healed of asthma at the crusade. He told me that as a journalist, Argimiro had invited him to accompany him on a plane ride over Colombo. Argimiro had piloted the single engine Cessna, circling over Colombo several times. Argimiro had kept fervently praying, sometimes with one hand raised to heaven, so much so that the journalist said he was afraid of the way the plane was flown. We now know this was a symbolic gesture praying in the heights above the clouds knowing that Satan is the Prince of the Power of the Air. (*Ephesians 2:2*). Now we know he had been binding satanic forces over the island before the Crusade began.

I could hardly wait to get back home to share the amazing news with Hildegard. There was no phone to call her on and tell of these things in advance. Reaching home, I burst into the room where Hildegard was and said, "Do you know what happened at the meetings?" I told her of the amazing miracles such as I had never before seen in my life.

The next few days were spent in reflection. How did Argimiro manage to do this? Was he particularly called and gifted with healing power? I had not seen a preacher who prayed a "mass prayer" and saw such astonishing results. He never laid his hands on anyone at the Park yet people were healed. This was a totally new technique or method which I thought would work with large crowds. I remember seeing Oral Roberts on films praying for the sick by the laying on of his hands which totally exhausted him. He had a smaller tent where the invalids were and after praying for the people who had lined up he went in there and prayed for them.

I began to pray and read the Gospels and the book of Acts. I read how Jesus went about teaching and healing people. I read how he cast out the deaf and dumb spirit with his Word. Jesus said that those who would believe in him would do the same works and greater works than those.

Read the book of Acts and you will see how Jesus' disciples did the same. The cripples walked, while the sick were healed when Peter's shadow fell on them. "And believers were increasingly added to the Lord, multitudes of both men and women, so that they brought the sick out into the streets and laid them on beds and couches, that at least the shadow of Peter passing by might fall on some of them." *(Acts 5:14-15)*

The Apostles also prayed that the Lord would send his healing power and they went forth and healed the sick them in the name of the anointed servant Lord Jesus. I meditated long on the verse in Acts 10.38, "how God anointed Jesus of Nazareth with the Holy Spirit and with power, who went about doing good and healing all who were oppressed by the devil, for God was with Him."

I read the Gospels to capture a clear picture of Jesus of Nazareth. I saw him overflowing with compassion and mercy to the sick and suffering. I read Hebrews 13:8, "Jesus Christ is the same yesterday, today, and forever." So, he has not changed and so we should witness the miracles he did when he was on the earth. With such assurance from the Scriptures, I told myself that I could do what Argimiro had done in Colombo.

* * *

Our son Mark was born at the end of March, 1972. We were now discussing how and when we could hold a mass healing crusade. The ideal place, we decided would be Jaffna; far away from people we knew and where any setback would not be noticed. Pastor Arumainayagam agreed to arrange an open air public meeting in Jaffna, during the August vacation which was ideal, since the LBI students could be there with us to assist.

In the meantime, we began to fast and pray along with the members of the church and students of the Bible School. These fasts lasted a few days and sometimes longer. Arumainayagam booked a sports ground belonging to the Sinhala Maha Vidyalaya in the heart of the town. During our prayer, Hildegard saw a vision and asked me whether fences in Jaffna are covered with palm branches. I told her the Jaffna Tamils live in very cloistered homes and all the fences are generously covered with dry palm branches so that passersby would not be able to see through to their homes. Several other visions were seen during prayer.

A large consignment of handbills were printed in Kandy using the same format of advertising that was used in Colombo. These were sent by train to Jaffna as soon as they were printed. The handbills proclaimed that Jesus

Christ is the answer to all life's problems. 'Jesus Lives!' and 'Jesus Saves!' were the subtitles. It also included texts instructing people to bring the blind, deaf and sick for prayer. The handbills also said that the greatest power on earth is the power of faith in God.

Somebody got hold of one of these handbills in Kandy and started teasing us. "Do you think you can do what Argimiro did in Colombo? Impossible!" he scoffed.

We arrived in Jaffna, checked into Palm Garden Hotel and met with Paul and his workers. Several of our students, along with Emmanuel who was leading the song service, arrived by train, while we drove from Kandy to Jaffna, taking with us our son Mark who was now six months old. There was no air-conditioning in the car and we had to stop at Vavuniya to place a cool towel on his body as we noticed his skin turning a reddish colour. The journey from Kandy to Jaffna is about 200 miles.

We arrived in Jaffna a few days prior to the crusade which was to begin on a Sunday and on Friday we drove to the Sports Ground of the school. As we came close, Hildegard was intently looking at the fences of houses and also the fences that were part of the ground. She turned to me and said, "These were the exact fences that I saw in my vision!"

Whew! The Spirit had shown her the very ground where the crusade was going to be held, while we had been yet in Kandy! This was another confirmation that we were in the perfect will of God.

The next day, we went to the ground itself and saw men building a platform at one end of the field. This was early in the morning and I saw them sawing and nailing planks on to a frame which was now resting on about 12 Palmyra tree trunks, cut so that the platform was about ten feet above the ground. As I was gazing on at this construction, a student tapped on my shoulder and told me that there was someone, who had already come from far, to the crusade. I turned and saw a man in his thirties with a travelling bag in his hands. I asked him from where he hailed and he replied, "All the way from Batticaloa, sir. I saw your advertisement in the newspaper. I am sick and I came to get healed."

I hoped to myself that he would be healed since, if not, this would be such a big disappointment for him after such a long journey.

Sunday night, the 23rd of August, was the first night of the meetings.

The Jaffna air was dry and the sun was slowly setting over the horizon. Jaffna is close to the beach and the air can be salty sometimes. I stayed at the hotel with Hildegard while the song service was going on. At around half past six, one of the workers reported that there were about four to five hundred people at the grounds. Feeling elated, we drove to the grounds, climbed the steps just behind the platform and took our seats.

As the singing continued, the crowd began to swell to about seven hundred or so. I was introduced and went to preach with one interpreter who translated my message into Tamil. I asked them, "Do you want to hear God's voice tonight?"

"Yes!" came the reply from the crowd.

"How can you hear the voice of God?" I lifted the Bible and said, "This Book is the Word and the Voice of God. This book declares that Jesus came to save and heal and deliver from all the power of Satan. If you believe, you will see the glory of the Lord!"

The altar call was given and hundreds raised their hands indicating that they wanted to receive Christ as their Saviour. Then we prayed for the healing of the sick. All our brothers fervently began to pray, as if their very life was dependent on this moment of prayer.

After prayer I asked whether anyone was healed, and if so, to please come up to the platform and tell us what happened. I waited and no one moved. Everyone was holding their breath. Suddenly, from my left, far away from the platform, a woman began to move. She stood up and cautiously began to walk towards us. She walked up the ramp came to the microphone and lifting her hand said, "Praise the Lord and praise the Lord! I was unable to walk for eighteen years. I felt the power of God and now I can walk! Praise the Lord!" She told us that her sons had brought her to the ground and left her there, hoping that she would be healed.

When she began to walk on the platform with upraised hands there was a murmur in the crowd. People were saying to each other, "Look! There is something happening here. This is real!"

People who stood far off in the crowd were now were inching up towards the platform wanting to get a closer glimpse of the miracle.

Next was a young deaf woman. She was tested like in Argimiro's crusade. She began to repeat a few words such as 'Amen' and 'Hallelujah' and 'Jesus', to the great amazement of the people. Now the crowd was all agog and knew a remarkable healing has taken place. Our Brothers were bringing more and more people forward who were now testifying that they were healed. Down at the bottom of the ramp our brothers were testing people who claimed to be healed and only genuine cases were sent up to testify.

Hildegard and I left the platform, walked to our car and drove to the hotel. We held each other's hands and just praised the Lord for that awesome day and for the things we had seen and heard.

Shortly after we arrived back at the hotel the workers came and told us of some others who came and testified of being healed. Our joy knew no bounds.

On the second night, over 3,000 were present. This happened to be a public holiday throughout the land. Christian's were praying for us. The Lord did great miracles that night. A young man had come to the field at seven in the morning. Danny, a team member had seen the boy with a badly deformed leg. That evening the power of the Lord hit him and he was instantly healed! Praise God! For nineteen years, he had been a cripple. The deaf had begun to hear and the dumb to talk... just like in the days of Jesus.

A man who had been sick with arthritis ran onto the platform, giving God the glory.

On the fourth day, about 10,000 had crowded onto the field. The sick and afflicted were brought in cars and laid near the platform. The heart melts in compassion when the sick and the suffering are laid before you in their helpless state.

Jesus said "I have come that they may have life, and that they may have it more abundantly." *(John 10:10)*

On the last day, over 20,000 were gathered. People were now seated so close to each other that they could not regain their seats when they stood. Our team of over sixty people did yeoman service assisting the various departments in the crusade. There were hardly any law officers, though we did have a few guards. How thankful and grateful we are to all who cheerfully helped us day and night in this outreach.

Just before the last service, Hildegard and I were in prayer. The Lord showed us a beautiful vision. The arm of Jesus was outstretched over a large multitude. They were reaching out to touch that great arm. This arm seemed to stretch out from the cross. The message was clear: "Tell the people to believe and I will do great things."

That night I went up on that platform energized by that vision. The field was a sea of heads and waving hands. What a glorious sight it was! That night, thousands prayed the sinner's prayer. It sounded like the rumble of distant thunder. We prayed for over 2,000 prayer requests brought to us in boxes. After a short message on the necessity of the New Birth, the sick were prayed for, again en masse. Immediately after the prayer, a stream of people who had been healed came up. Mothers brought their children, the deaf began to hear and the dumb spoke.

One mother said that her child had been healed on the first day but she had not testified. A few days later, the sickness had come back. She had then decided to testify. The child began to improve as she prayed.

One man came up. He had been a leper. He told us that the power of God had hit him and that all his racking pains had vanished. How thrilled we were! Only a few hours earlier, we had asked the Lord for a special anointing to cure the sick with skin diseases and on Saturday, this man came to Deliverance Hall and he proclaimed that he now felt the blood flowing through his limbs. He was now able to move his fingers and wanted to be baptized. Hallelujah! Jesus is the same, yesterday, today and forever! Jesus of Nazareth is Jesus of Jaffna too.

The crowds were so great that every morning, two convert classes had to be held. On Sunday, Brother Paul had to have four services in his church to accommodate the crowd. Nearly thirty people were baptized in the Holy Spirit and plans were made for a large baptismal service the next month. God is indeed good.

I will never forget what happened one particular night. As we got into the car to leave a meeting, a young man came up. He looked into our car with his face shining, showing us his ears. He said, rather haltingly, "I can hear... I can hear..."

Our hearts are humbled. We are deeply moved as we see the mighty arm of Jesus touching the sick and the afflicted. We want to go on and on and on... No man can remain the same having see Jesus in action.

The Jaffna Crusade is now history. The platform is dismantled and the crowds have gone away. Emptiness rules the once-crowded field, but the spiritual impact still reverberates in the peninsula.

Never in the history of Jaffna had 20,000 people gathered in one place to listen to a preacher and see great miracles done in the name of Jesus. Never before had the air of Jaffna been rent with the voices of 15,000 people, praising God, on seeing the cripples walk and the dumb speak.

For ten glorious days, ONE PERSON was the HERO in Jaffna... JESUS. Everyone knew about Jesus. Scores of Hindus came to the platform and boldly testified before the multitudes, that JESUS had healed them.

Many had warned that Jaffna was a tradition-bound land. Christianity was associated with a section of society that went to church on Sunday. Jesus was a good teacher and a good man... that was all. We had advertised that we would pray for the blind, the deaf and the dumb in the name of Jesus, and in response, they had now gathered.

The following are excerpts from a letter written by Arumainayagam on the Jaffna Crusade:

> "Praise the Lord Jesus Christ for His wonderful guidance in arranging a Salvation-Healing Crusade at Jaffna from the 23rd August to the 1st September, 1972.
>
> "This was the first Christian Mass Crusade at Jaffna where thousands of people of all faiths came together in the name of the Lord Jesus Christ and God did great things in our midst in the North of Sri Lanka. On the 10th day there were more than 20 to 25 thousand people anxiously waiting to hear God's message. This reminded us of the Bible days, when thousands of people gladly received Jesus Christ as Saviour and Lord. Souls were saved and healed by God's power. Hundreds of blind, deaf and dumb people were wonderfully delivered by the power of God. So many heart cases were healed. The crippled were able to walk.
>
> "This is only a very short report of the great things God did in Jaffna. From three thousand, the number grew to nearly 25 thousand within those ten days and still people are coming for healing prayers. Now the meetings are held in the Deliverance Hall. Please pray that God will send in more labourers into this field. Please pray for us."

Today, Zion Church Jaffna has around 4,000 believers and twenty Branch Churches and is led by Pastor Josiah. The church is an integral part of the Fellowship of Free Churches of Sri Lanka.

17

Chilaw Mass Crusade. Miracles and Healings. The Vision of the Outstretched Arm with the Streak of Fire. The Vision of the Mighty Angel Standing Over the Multitudes. The Crusades Extends Two More Days. Bro. Henry de Silva is Called to Remain in Chilaw.

DECEMBER 28, JUST AFTER CHRISTMAS OF 1972, AND THEREON FOR ten days ending on the 4th of January 1973, saw another Mass Healing Crusade in the city of Chilaw.

Chilaw is situated fifty miles north of Colombo, a peaceful city with broad, sandy beaches on the north-western seaboard. Most of the inhabitants earn their livelihood by fishing. At dawn, the day's catch is unloaded, the fishing boats securely anchored, and the whole family is busy cleaning and mending nets, making ready for the morrow.

A few miles from the Chilaw rest house stands the famous Munneswaram temple, a Hindu "holy place" to which many thousands of pilgrims come throughout the year to perform their *poojas*[1] and pay their vows. The road is lined with hundreds of huts, erected to provide shelter to the lost multitudes that come seeking peace with God.

The prospect of holding a Mass Crusade in Chilaw had brought great thrill to our hearts, but we soon discovered that we did not know one believer in that area who would assist us. We went ahead, nevertheless, in the assurance that God is *Jehovah-Jireh* – the One who will Provide.

We found many friends and others who helped us. Our every need was

[1] A *Pooja* is a religious ritual performed as an offering to various deities.

met by the Providence of God. Praise His Holy Name!

On arrival, the Team slid smoothly into the task, fanning out into the suburbs to do a blanket cover of the area. Fifty thousand handbills had to be distributed and 2,000 posters displayed all over the city and suburbs. Two teams worked from dusk till dawn to put up the red and white posters along the main thoroughfare from Negombo to Chilaw.

When we arrived in Chilaw we knew we were on the verge of a great visitation! Ours would be the first Mass Crusade ever held in this city. By sunset on opening day, the large football field had become hallowed, holy ground, where, for the next ten days, the Blessed Holy Spirit would minister healing to hundreds of afflicted ones, both body and soul.

Beyond the cordoned off platform area, stood hundreds of people of all faiths and all walks of life. Those who were seriously sick were seated on the floor. As usual, there were a large number of children brought for prayer.

On the first night there were about a thousand people present. The Message of the Gospel was preached and over 600 people prayed the sinner's prayer that night, giving their hearts to Jesus.

Then we began to pray for the sick. The first one to come up on the platform and testify was a man who had been deaf in one year for several years. He was carefully tested, and from the platform he told the people how the Lord had healed him. The next one was an elderly man who had been suffering from an acute pain in the back. Up on the platform, he demonstrated that he could now walk, pain-free.

The people knew now that they were going to witness great things over the next few days. They had experienced only a foretaste of the great blessings in store for them.

The next few days saw a tremendous spiritual breakthrough. On the third night, a young Moslem lady came up and testified that she had been healed of deafness. A young boy, unable to walk, was brought to the meeting, carried by his father. After prayer, he was wonderfully healed and was seen walking briskly back and forth on the platform. The Power of the Lord was present to heal and to deliver. Several testified that they had been delivered from the power of evil spirits. For the first time in its history, the vast football field resonated with the voice of the multitudes, praising God.

While in prayer before the Crusade, the Lord had shown to us in a vision, an outstretched arm marked with a streak of fire on it. During the ten days, of the Crusade, many who had ailments on their limbs, especially the arms, received healing.

One night, just before the service, the Lord showed us, in a vision, a mighty angel standing in triumph over the multitudes. Oh! It was indeed a glorious meeting that night. Thousands responded to the call and came forward to receive the Lord. That night, the Lord once again confirmed His Word with signs and miracles. Several who were suffering from horrible skin diseases were healed. Many were restored to health.

Each morning, over 100 people were now attending the Faith Class in the pavilion. Throughout the day, large numbers visited the field. Our workers had a blessed time in personal counselling and sharing Christ with these visitors. Under deep conviction, through the preached Word of God, people were now giving up evil things like cigarettes, charms and amulets in their possession. One night, a knife was placed on the platform! The Lord had spoken and someone had surrendered this implement.

Daily attendance had now reached the 9,000 mark. Due to popular request, it was decided to extend the Crusade for two more days. The Lord very wonderfully confirmed this decision. On the tenth day, over fifty people were instantaneously healed, following the mass prayer. Testimonies of those that had been healed continued far into the night; long after we had left the field.

God is a good God. "He loved the world so much that He sent His Son Jesus, and whosoever believeth in Him shall never perish but have everlasting life..." Abundant Life... Now!

Brother Henry de Silva felt the call of God to stay behind in Chilaw to continue in the ministry of compassion; to help in the establishing of New Testament Church in accordance with the Word of God. The church was christened the Bethlehem Church, since it was born during Christmas. Pastor Yogarajah is the pastor of the church, and he has brought healing and deliverance to many.

Today, the church is large enough to hold 900 people, being extended three times to date. It also has twenty branch churches. The original property was bought with the donations of the young people of Rudy Schwabe's Church (Hildegard's home church in Germany). The property was purchased for Rs. 25,000.

We are grateful, for as we followed Jesus, he has made us fishers of men in Chilaw, Sri Lanka.

18

Our Move to Pasadena. McGavran's Theory. Paul Yonggi Cho's 'Five'. Wagner and Wimber. Charisma Arrives in Fuller Seminary. The Third Wave.

AT THE END OF 1979, HILDEGARD AND I, ALONG WITH OUR THREE sons, Mark, who was seven, Stephan, five and Dennis, our youngest at three, settled down in Pasadena, California. I had been accepted into Fuller Seminary to follow a M.A. in Missiology (now called Inter-Cultural studies). On New Year's Day, 1980, we were witness to the world famous Rose Parade, a festival of flower-covered floats and marching bands celebrating the New Year. I began attending lectures at Fuller right after.

The Fuller Theological Seminary was founded by Charles Fuller in 1947. It is the largest interdenominational Seminary in the world.[1] Currently it has an enrolment of over 4,300 students from 67 countries and 100 denominations. It offers degrees in Theology, Psychology and Missiology, (ICS). The Library has over 50,000 books shelved in a building four storey's tall. What a privilege it was to mentor under renowned gurus of Church Growth such as Donald McGavran, Peter Wagner and Chuck Kraft, just to mention a few.

During winter break, I was speaking to a prominent Charismatic leader in Texas. She knew me and my work in Sri Lanka and expressed surprise that I had selected a Liberal Seminary to follow my graduate studies. I

[1] *Ref:* George M. Marsden, (1987). "*Reforming Fundamentalism: Fuller Seminary and the New Evangelicalism*". Grand Rapids: William B. Eerdmans Publishing. ISBN 978-0-8028-3642-7.

told her, "Many Liberals are human beings with a hunger for the supranatural and Fuller needs an outpouring of the Holy Spirit. I hope it will happen there during my time."

Some of my lecturers at Fuller were Donald McGavran and Paul Hiebert who were missionaries in India, Charles Kraft in Africa and Peter Wagner in South America. They were intellectual men of the highest calibre, yet modest and unassuming.

At Fuller, with the help of these men, I was able to expand my world view by understanding cultures and how to communicate the Gospel in such terms that the receptor understood the message. In Anthropology, we were taught to understand the process of conversion and the reality of the Power Encounter. There was great emphasis on growing churches by identifying homogenous units. McGavran taught that Churches will grow and multiply if the convert does not need to cross cultural and language barriers. Through extensive research, McGavran explained how churches grew when they recognized the "Bridges of God", that is, the conversion of the whole, or the aim to win whole families and not selected individuals.

McGavran's theory was proven as Churches grew in India and multiplied. Wagner began to adapt these principles to the American and Western Churches. He wrote extensively on dynamic factors that promote Church Growth. Thousands of Dissertations were accepted by Fuller from Third World and First World Doctoral students who proved, in their writings, that the principles enunciated by McGavran and Company worked in their own cultural setting.

My M.A. Thesis was on *"Discipling the Moslems of Sri Lanka"*, followed by my Doctoral Dissertation entitled *"Planting Churches among Hindu Tamils in Sri Lanka"*. I learnt that one of the main reasons why the Hindu family vehemently opposes the conversion of their eldest son is because, when the father dies, the eldest son has to perform certain *"Poojas"* that will ensure the father does not go to hell. The son is called *"Putran"*, meaning 'one who delivers from hell'. Imagine how the Hindus would despise the Church which converted their son, thus depriving the father of *"Moksha"* or union with the Brahama.

For my research on my dissertation, I sent out 300 questionnaires to Hindus who had applied to enrol in the Bible Correspondence Course.

One question was, 'which is the greatest sin: adultery, murder, theft or the killing of a cow?' Almost all responded saying the greatest sin is the killing of a cow. In the cosmological theory of the Hindu belief, the division between God, Angels, Man and Animals is blurred. *'Hanuman'* (the monkey) and the Cobra are objects of worship and veneration.

I visited several Hindu Temples and engaged in conversation with *kurakul* or priests and discovered how they perceived the world, the universe, life after death, and Christian Churches. This is so important, if communication is to be effective.

I also had access to bound volumes of correspondence between the Missionaries who belonged to the American Board of Foreign Missions from as far back as the late 1880's, up to 1947. Hundreds of American Missionaries served in Jaffna during this period and over forty missionary children died and were buried in the north of Sri Lanka within a period of thirty years. John Foster Dulles, former Secretary of State, when he visited Sri Lanka in the early fifties had indicated that he would like to visit his grandfather's grave in Jaffna. His grandfather was a Missionary who had served and died in Jaffna. The Sri Lankan government complied with his request and provided a plane for him to fly to Jaffna.

Most of the conversions in that period were through schools and medical missions. One of Sri Lanka's greatest Preachers was Dr. D. T. Niles, whose father was a convert from Hinduism. The father's name was D. P. Niles which stood for Daniel Poor Niles. Poor was a well-respected American Doctor who started a Mission Hospital in Manipay, Jaffna.

During my research, I read about a "revival" that broke out in a girl's school in Manipay. Many were converted and turned to the Lord. Such events then were rare and few. As I read of the immense sacrifice and suffering many endured only to see such limited results, I wondered what would have happened if the missionaries had held a few mass healing Crusades as we had done in 1972, in Jaffna, in those early years. I am convinced that, if they had done so, there would have been a far greater number of Christians in Jaffna than there are today.

While in Fuller, our sons studied at the local schools, were members of the Junior Leagues, and Hildegard worked as Secretary to the Director of the Psychology Department. My Brother-in-Law, David Ephraim and

Roshan arrived in Pasadena shortly before we left for Sri Lanka. He, too, earned his doctoral degree from the Fuller Seminary.

My father had taught me that the easiest thing to carry around is prayer. I now carried my prayer ministry into the sprawling 100 million dollar campus in Oakland, Pasadena, California. The Palm-fringed sidewalks became my prayer lanes. The Chapel, which was very sparingly used, was now my Garden of Prayer. I had seen the Spirit move in Bethesda Hall, and in BFC, and in signs and wonders in our crusades in answer to prayer and intercession. I was convinced that a similar awakening awaited the Fuller Pasadena Campus.

The 1980's were characterized by prodigious interest in Church Growth. One of the impetuses for this unprecedented interest in Church Growth was the phenomenal growth of the Yoido Full Gospel Church whose Pastor was Paul Yonggi Cho from South Korea. His church, in the mid-seventies, had 20,000 members and was rapidly growing. By 1980 it had several hundred thousand members and today, is the largest church in the world, with nearly a million members.

I remember meeting Cho in 1974 in Seoul Korea and he told me there are five important things in growing a church. First, he said, was prayer, second: sound biblical preaching, third: home cells, fourth: giving, and fifth: tithing. Needless to say, in our ministry, we have endeavoured to follow these principles of growth and it has certainly helped.

Yonggi Cho's church growth began to impact many nations of the world. Pastors saw that the self-imposed ceiling limit was now shattered by a converted Korean preacher, and Pastor's began to pray and concentrated on growing the Church. McGavran and Wagner were now the Theoreticians of church growth, and Cho its famous Practitioner, and this trio were destined to make a pronounced impact on the Christian Church World.

In 1982, John Wimber entered the stage. He was a pop musician – now converted – and was the founder of the Vineyard Churches. Wimber was invited to teach a course entitled *"Signs and Wonders and Church Growth"* at Fuller Seminary. This course was open to all three schools of Fuller and the enrolment for this course was over 130 students. I too signed up for the course, 'MC 510: Signs and Wonders and Church Growth.'

The first night, the lecture hall was packed and extra chairs had to be placed at the back. Usually the highest enrolment is for courses that the President David Hubbard offered. Some of the Professors were standing, observing rather curiously, listening to the lectures. Among them was Chuck Kraft who later wrote a book on Power Healing.[2] (He was a Brethren Missionary in Nigeria and prayed for stunted legs and arms to be lengthened.)

Wimber explained the Biblical foundation of signs and wonders, both from the Old and New Testament. He also showed a video clip of William Branham calling out people by name and address in a crusade in New York, the first time I ever saw one. I had only read about him in books.

Wimber then said he was now going to pray. Immediately we closed our eyes and bent our heads, expecting him to start praying. "Don't close your eyes. Look up and see what God is going to do" he said in a very conversational style.

Now this was unusual and unconventional. This was a real laid-back style that was so different to the Pentecostals and Charismatic's to some extent. As we watched, an unseen wave of power seemed to descend on the lecture room. Within minutes some of the students slowly slid to the ground very gently, others were shaking and trembling. Some were moaning and others were weeping. Several of these students were from the school of Theology and Psychology who were distrustful of healing and manifestations of the Holy Spirit. This wave continued for over an hour and hardly anyone left the hall. I was later told that some stayed until midnight, even though the classes had begun at seven that evening. Charismata had invaded Fuller Seminary, a conservative and evangelical seminary, for the first time since its inception in 1947. The visitation that I and others had prayed for was now happening in 1982, the second year of my studies at the Seminary.

The Course "Signs and Wonders and Church Growth" was now offered and taught in many Seminaries across America. What appealed to Conservatives and Evangelicals was the "laid back" style of Wimber's teaching and praying for the sick. The Word of Knowledge and the Word

---

2 *Ref:* Charles H. Kraft: (1997) *"I Give You Authority: Practicing the Authority Jesus Gave Us"*. Chosen Books. ISBN 13: 9780800792565

of Wisdom operated regularly in Wimber's lectures and Teachings.

Both Wimber and Wagner gave rise to a breath of fresh air that was neither fully Pentecostal nor even charismatic in its operation. Eventually this movement was called the "Third Wave of the Holy Spirit". This movement began to highlight the importance of Preaching the Gospel with attestation and power. Wimber and Wagner began to teach that God is rising up Apostolic Ministers and the new Prophets and Apostles would perform miracles similar to what was found in the book of Acts in greater intensity and quantity.

Wagner was a prolific writer whose early books were on Church Growth with emphasis on the US landscape. Later, he began to write several books on Spiritual Warfare. The best sellers among them were *Confronting the Powers* (Regal Books, Ventura CA, 1993), and *Breaking Your Strongholds in Our City* (Regal Books, Ventura CA, 1991).

Wagner believes that Satan has high-ranking evil spirits that are assigned to control nations, regions, peoples groups, social networks, and political authorities. There are world rulers who execute the decree of Satan. Their work is to prevent the conversion of people to Christ. When these powers are overcome through prayer, fasting and intercession, people are released and set free.

Jesus had said when you bind the strong man then you can spoil his goods. Jesus said, "When the strong man, fully armed, guards his own dwelling, his belongings are undisturbed. But when one stronger than he attacks him and conquers him, he robs him of his whole armour on which he had relied and divides up and distributes all his goods as plunder." *(Luke 11:21-22 – Amplified Bible)*

Wagner explained that a different level of warfare among the highest is cosmic warfare where the invisible despotic powers of Satan are bound and made impotent *(see Daniel 10 and Ephesians 6).* St. Paul asserts that our warfare is not with flesh and blood but with invisible supra-natural powers in the heavenlies.

In the following chapter I will relate an incident that occurred on our visit to Dubai in the UAE that demonstrates the reality of these powers, that are holding nations and people in bondage.

19

Invitations to Dubai. Healing Waters in the Palace of the Sheik. Intercessory Prayer and Healing Pseudomonas in Germany.

I had always had a burden in my heart to preach the Gospel in the Arab world. In 1996, while I was still the Pastor of Lighthouse Church, some of the brethren, including Terry Jones, assembled to pray for the United Arab Republic and in particular, for Dubai, since I had received an invitation to come to that city for ministry.

Dubai is a city state in the United Arab Emirates. It was formally established in 1833 by Sheik Maktoum Bin Al-Maktoum. It is city state, and the cosmopolitan cultural hub of the Middle East. About seventeen percent of its population is Arab. A large number of Asians live and work here. The GDP in 2008 was $82 billion.

Islam is the official religion of this state. Almost all mosques are funded, and imams are paid, by the Government. There are large numbers of Christians, Sikhs, Buddhist and Hindus. Christians are allowed to worship in a Church or its premises, provided it is authorized by the Government. No proselytizing is allowed and distributing religious literature is strictly forbidden; a crime punishable by imprisonment or deportation.

Despite these boundaries placed on the spreading of the Gospel, in 2010 we were able to telecast our *Miracle Service* TV program to over 35 Middle Eastern countries, from a Television Studio located in Cyprus.

Before our journey and during a time of prayer, Rohan Johnson saw in a vision us carrying water to the desert; a welcome confirmation of our intended journey to Dubai.

In the meantime, Monica, a member of our Poornawatte Lighthouse Church, in Kandy and employed in the home of a Sheik and his family, had invited us as well. The Sheik's family knew Monica to be a Christian and she had the love and respect of the household. Whenever someone was sick, they would ask Monica to pray for them, which she did gladly.

A time came when the eldest daughter complained of inability to sleep and the mother had severe pain in her body which continued unabated for a long time. Monica told them of the priests in her church who pray for the sick and how many had been cured. She invited us to come to Dubai when possible and said we would be most welcome to visit them for prayer.

I received an invitation to come and speak at Kings Revival Church in Dubai, pastored by V. Dilkumar. This is the largest congregation in the UAE. Dilkumar told me he first heard the Gospel in our Wednesday Youth Fellowship in Kandy when he was a student at the Peradeniya University, even though he did not get saved then.

I travelled to Dubai with Saman, who knew Monica well, and we were met by a family who were part of the Lighthouse Church. Anne, the eldest daughter of Rajamoney, was a very active figure in the church and accompanied us during our stay in Dubai.

When we shared the invitation to visit the home of the Sheik, with friends of ours, the church was shocked and warned us that it would be very dangerous to go and pray for them. They cautioned that we were visitors and did not know the ground realities of the Muslim world. They feared we might be imprisoned if we were to go and pray, especially for the womenfolk, when the men were absent.

Hearing this, we were somewhat apprehensive and delayed our trip for a few days. Monica called and inquired as to why we were delaying? "The family is waiting for your visit, please come soon." We told her that we would come the next morning and asked her to make arrangements to pick us up.

The next morning, as instructed by her, we waited near the church. Right on time, a Benz car with Arabic numeral plates pulled up. Only Sheiks were allowed to have this special number.

Beckoning us to get into the car was Monica, well dressed with a few gold chains adorning her neck. A short drive saw us arriving at the palace of the Sheik. The Sheik, to our relief, was away in another country. His wife Tarifa, her sister, Halima, her mother and her very attractive daughter who was a university student and also the youngest daughter of the Sheik were in the house.

We were very cordially welcomed and led to the living room. The carpets were so thick and beautifully woven, that one hesitated to walk on such luxurious material. Tea and fruits were served, along with the most sweet, mouth-watering and delicious dates.

After a brief introduction, Saman, Anne and I sat on a sofa and told them to come and sit on the carpet before us as we were going to pray. We sang the chorus, "There is power, power, wonder-working power" in Sinhala a few times and the atmosphere began to change as we felt the presence of Jesus in that room. We also began to speak in tongues and although that sound may have been strange to them, it must have evoked a sense of the supernatural associated with us.

Then I called for some oil and somewhat cautiously handed the bottle to Anne, instructing her to anoint all the ladies present. You could only imagine if we broke protocol and laid our hands on their heads! We prayed fervently and every rebuke and binding of the evil spirit was done in Sinhala! After this session of prayer, they seemed very delighted and happy that we had come and we took time to pray for them. I also believe that Jesus promised us that he will always be with us wherever we are.

A wonderful peace pervaded the place where we were seated. We were served with more fruits and dates and not much later, took our leave, not before acquiring Anne's telephone number to keep in touch.

The person most overjoyed was Monica. She was proud of how we handled the situation. The next day, we got a call, "Please come and pray again." On this visit, we were feeling quite at home. This time around we were bold enough to lay our hands on each of the women while praying for them. We received more gifts and fruits on this visit as well.

That evening, while walking along the streets of Dubai, Anne's phone began to ring, "Anne, bring your friends for prayer tomorrow. Do not fail." The next day we were picked up by the same chauffer, this time friendlier than before.

Again we sat down. Tarifa was seated on the sofa while her sister Halima was seated on the ground. She told us her husband had gone away and she was unhappy with him. We began to sing and prayed for every one of them. No sooner had we finished praying, when Tarifa gave out a squeak and sat up from the sofa. "Oh. I felt something in my back! The pain has left me and I am free… free!"

She said that nine years ago, when she had delivered her daughter, there was an indentation on her pelvic bone and it had caused her pain when she turned or got up from the seat. Needless to say, we were thrilled that Jesus had graciously touched her.

Now Halima spoke. She said Sheika, her daughter around twenty years of age, an attractive girl, had not been able to sleep peacefully for several years. In the night she would wake up to the terrifying feeling that somebody was behind the bed and about to touch her! The last two nights she slept soundly and her night terrors had disappeared. We all said a loud 'Hallelujah!' and thanked the Lord for this wonderful answer to prayer.

Later, Saman told me that when the woman yelped, he saw a dark figure leaving her body. A spirit of infirmity had left her and she was free. Jesus, when he healed the woman who was bent for eighteen years, told the onlookers that she, a daughter of Abraham was bound by Satan and he had set her free.

Sheika, who was observing us carefully, and spoke flawless English, asked me how many times they should pray. I thought for a moment and realized that we were in the house of Muslims who pray five times a day. I told her to pray thrice – morning, noon and in the evening. She was very pleased and now wanted to know how to pray. I asked her for a paper and wrote a prayer to God for salvation in Jesus's name and for protection and blessing for the whole family.

More gifts, including some money, were given to us and we wished them goodbye and left the house rejoicing. Yes we did come with some apprehension, but left whistling *"Amazing Grace"* for all what the Lord had done. We indeed had brought Living Water to the desert. As we drove out of the palace gardens the date trees on either side of the alleyway were laden with large bunches of juicy ripe dates!

Later, we went to Monica's home and she spread the table with the most mouth-watering meal for which we thanked her profusely. She also told us that the sheik has fifty cars and one hundred servants to take care of his herds of the sheep, cows and camels.

* * *

Back in Kandy, not long after we returned from the miracles in the Arabian desert, Hildegard developed an itching in her right ear. We made an appointment with an ENT surgeon. He took one look inside Hildegard's ear and told us to go to Germany immediately for treatment.

The University Hospital in Tübingen, Germany, is very famous and patients came from far and wide for treatment there. We were confident that a doctor there would cure this infection speedily. Also, living in the neighbouring city of Reutlingen made travel very easy.

After a brief examination, the doctor prescribed some ointment to be applied to the cavity in the ear. Several days later, the itching persisted and we became anxious. We returned to the hospital and this time, the doctor gave her a more thorough and lengthier examination and suggested she come back for minor surgery. The smear had shown that her ear had been infected by the Pseudomonas bacteria (PB in short).

Pseudomonas is an aerobic bacteria and very slimy. There are 191 strains of it and they tend to make colonies inside any niche in the body. Some species secrete a yellow-green watery substance.

On the day of the surgery, Hildegard was taken to the ward and a slit was made near the opening of the ear. The ear was scraped out and bandaged. The surgery was over quickly over and I returned home while Hildegard remained in the ward for the night. The next day, I went to see her. The cut was bandaged but the ear was kept open. Strangely, a few days later, the itching and the discharge had begun again. We knew at once that the operation was not successful. Hildegard went back a few times but further treatment was not successful. We waited for another day and yet the oozing from the ear had not abated. This was now very serious. If the discharge was not checked, the watery substance could create an alien mass inside the labyrinth between both the ears and cause severe imbalance and even death.

The situation seemed grave but what could we do? I had to return to Sri Lanka, as one of the boys was alone at home in Kandy. I promised her that as soon as I got back, I would mobilize prayer in our church.

Our home, which was once a bright happy spot in Piachaud Gardens, was now a somewhat depressed place. I saw a picture of a cow that lost its balance mechanism; it was stumbling around in circles, unable to control itself. The inner ear aids the system of balance in both the man and animals.

Hildegard decided to consult a specialist in her town of Reutlingen. He was a top professor of ENT at the local hospital. He was very keen to treat this kind of unusual infection and listened to her describe her aliment. She underwent his treatment but, again, to no effect. He then told her that he was leaving for a medical congress in India soon and that she should consult with his assistant, for further treatment.

Hildegard was very discouraged, especially since, while in prayer, she had a definite impression that this was the doctor she should go to, and now he was leaving for India. Hopes were shattered.

Coming away from the doctor's office, she aimlessly walked the streets of Reutlingen, holding back the tears until she gained enough composure to go back home to tell her parents, who were anxiously watching and praying for her.

The only alternative was to meet this junior doctor, a short-term replacement, when she came in. She would only attend to the most serious cases left behind in the professor's absence. In the meantime I had appealed to everyone to pray for Hildegard. Many were the voices that were lifted up in prayer for her healing.

Now close to our home in Kandy, there was a lady who was a prayer warrior – Sister Pearl Nathaniels. She was a long standing member of our church and a regular member of the ladies prayer meetings. We occasionally met for prayer in her home.

One night, while we were praying very specially for Hildegard, Sister Pearl Nathaniels saw in a vision a huge boot coming down on a colony of microorganisms. The entire mass was crushed and destroyed.

Back in Germany, Hildegard went and met this junior doctor. As she entered, she heard these words, as she had so many times before, "I think we have an answer."

The junior doctor sounded very hopeful. "You have gone through a terrible time, but there is a new drug on the market. It has just been tested and we will have it in a couple of days. It is already being used in the USA and has been very successful."

In the meantime, I wrote to our friend, Dr. Bob Miller in Tulsa, and asked him whether there was a drug available for PB in America. He replied in the affirmative, gave me the name of the drug and promised to send me a sample if needed.

The medicine arrived and drops were applied to the inner ear. For a few days, the inner ear remained dry, but no sooner the treatment stopped the symptoms were back.

Hildegard was devastated. The medication was not working. The young lady doctor was shocked and immediately contacted the research centre. She was told that the slimy micro-organisms were retreating and hiding under the skin when the medication was applied only to come out in all force the moment the treatment ceased.

The answer was a more intense treatment with both ear drops and oral medication. After a few days, Hildegard knew without a doubt that the treatment had worked and the healing had started.

She booked her ticket back to Sri Lanka and took her last dose of medicine on the plane. Praise God for such a wonderful healing. This was a true miracle.

Prayer and intercession led her to meet the right doctor who had access to the right medication for the virus. Prayer and more prayer is the key to victory. Behind bacteria and disease-causing infection, fungus and yeast, there could be lurking an evil spirit who is bent on destroying God's wonderful creation. But when we launch spiritual war against them, they can be eliminated in the name of Jesus.

Hildegard was not only cured, but also helped several others find medical help too. It was reported that many people around the world, unable to find a cure for PB, had lost their lives or limbs. There was much rejoicing in the church when she returned and never again did she have a relapse.

20

Returning to Colombo. Founding of the New Covenant Church. The Wedding of Mark and Shania on 1.1.2000. Mark, Stephan and Dennis. The Patmos Media Ministry. The "Elephant Boy". Hope Angel Medical Clinics. Recovery of our Lost Passports through Gifts of the Spirit in Trichy, India. The Satellite Connection, the Christmas Programme and the Start of the Sky Media.

A FEW MONTHS BEFORE THE END OF THE YEAR 2000, WE MOVED to Colombo from Kandy and rented a house in Torrington Ave, Colombo 7. Colombo is both the political and economic capital of Sri Lanka. The origin of Colombo can be traced to the 5th century when it was a way station between the East and West. Three colonial powers, the Portuguese, the Dutch and the British occupied it and made it the Capital City.

One of the oldest churches in the city is the Wolfendhal, a church in Pettah, and services are held even today in this church. The floor is made up of tombstones from a Dutch Church in Fort. It was moved there in 1813.

The Scots Kirk, built for Scottish Tea Planters in 1842, is the most popular Church for weddings for many Christians. St. Peter's Church was previously the Banquet Hall of the Dutch Governor. Its city population is about one million but daily 40,000 light vehicles enter the city every working day, making it one of the most congested cities in the island.

The two largest Pentecostal/Charismatic churches, namely the Peoples' Church (Assembly of God) and the Calvary Church, are in Colombo city.

The Peoples' Church was founded by Pastor Dr. Colton Wickramaratne, a preacher whose delivery is as powerful as Malinga's[1] bowling and the Senior Pastor of Calvary Church (former Biblical Free Church) is Pastor Dr. Tissa Weerasinghe, a renowned bible expositor and an International Conference Speaker. Both these churches have a history of over fifty years.

There are over 20 million people living in the island. The Buddhists make up the majority of the population at 70 percent, Hindus at 12 percent, Moslems 9 percent and Christians, including the Catholics, are 7 percent. The Protestants number less than one percent of the population. Among them, Evangelical Christians may be less than 80,000 in Colombo. No accurate statistics are available. It is reported that although Colombo is called a garden city, nearly forty percent of its population lives in slums or conditions akin to slums. The compulsion to reach the masses of Colombo and Sri Lanka was the reason for our re-location from Kandy to Colombo.

After our arrival, we held the first service in our home with five people. They included Mark, Shania and Ranjit. We began to pray and seek the Lord in May 2000. As attendance increased, we moved to the fourth floor of the Cargill's Food City in Thimbirigasyaya. Later, as the congregation grew, we rented the fifth floor of the same building for our offices and Sunday school activities.

The New Covenant Church had its first service in the Food City hall and a small advertisement was placed in the *"Island"* paper advertising our Sunday Service. On Wednesday, an officer came to see us from the Colombo Municipality, with a letter from the Municipal Commissioner. A letter had been addressed to him by the Secretary of a Religious Organization that we had started an unauthorized Fellowship and it would disturb the peaceful atmosphere of the neighbourhood, with our loud preaching and prayers. We told the officer that we were there to pray for the nation, its leaders and for peace which is a desperate need of the land. Furthermore, we had air-conditioned and sound-proofed the hall so that we would not disturb any one of our neighbours. Samidu, one of our Brothers, took the officer down to the road and asked, "Can you hear any sound?" The drums and organ was played at full volume. He replied,

[1] Lasith Malinga is the name of the fast test bowler of the Sri Lanka cricket team

"I can't hear any sound. It is very good."

Samidu took him upstairs and asked him, "Can I pray for you?"

"Please do," he replied.

When Samidu prayed, the Word of Knowledge began to operate which revealed specifics of his family problems which were troubling him. The officer asked whether he could come for our services to which we replied, "You are most welcome."

We never heard from him since. It must be borne in mind that this was a a period which was very hostile to Christians. In the mid-nineties, a number of churches were attacked and pews and other furniture destroyed. We were glad that we had, on arrival, air-conditioned the church hall.

Buddhists go to the temples to meditate and hear a sermon; a temple is a very silent and serene place with no music or singing. The loud singing and praising in some of the churches has generated an aversion to the manner in which churches conduct their services, especially on Sundays, when people sleep late and are at home. This is one reason for the opposition to churches and the erection of new churches in the city as well as in towns and villages.

As services continued at the Food City auditorium, we witnessed an increase in the attendance each Sunday. The services now were held in Sinhala, Tamil and English at three different times on Sundays. The Sunday school too began to grow and new children were added. We held three baptismal services in three different churches as we had no tank to baptize the new converts in.

There was a remarkable incident that took place several years ago at the Food City. A young engineer arrived from England, whose mother is a member of our church. His father is a reputed orthopaedic surgeon who has treated Sultans in the Emirates. He came forward to be prayed for at the close of the service. I laid my hands on him and prayed a simple prayer. Later he told me, as I was praying, something happened to him. He saw the face of Jesus for just about twenty seconds. It was a kindly face, and he looked at the young man and vanished. He told me he can never ever forget that exhilarating experience and it was indeed life changing. Today, he is back in the island as a senior project manager for a British company. He and his mother attend church regularly. We are humbled that the Lord has used such unworthy servants to bring salvation to others.

* * *

We celebrated the dawn of the 3rd Millennium with the marriage of our eldest son, Mark, and Shania McFarlin. Their marriage was registered at the Mount Lavinia Hotel with our close relatives and friends. Since they were hoping to return to America, we had the ceremony on the first of January, 2000.

We had just moved to Colombo and decided to have a simple ceremony and celebration in Colombo. They were preparing to have a church wedding later on in Wisconsin where Shania's relatives were. The same year, Shania and Mark flew to Wisconsin and we, too, attended the church wedding along with her relatives and friends.

Shania had several miraculous healings in her life and Mark and Shania now have a son Gabriel Andreas – our first grandson.

Dennis studied and lives in Tulsa. Dennis, in 2004, came back home and organised a medical clinic in Pothupitiya in the hill-country. His heart of compassion was moved when he saw the great needs of the mothers, children and so many sick people. Afterwards he went to his former Hebron school in Ooti[2] and visited the Taj Mahal. On his return he was suffering with a severe stomach ailment and began losing weight. Doctors in the USA and Germany were unable to diagnose the root cause of the infection. Gastro paralysis was the end diagnosis. We were close to losing our beloved son, but God intervened. Prayer and his tenacity to overcome this deadly infection has seen him restored to health.

During this time we had been closely associated with Harvest Church, Tulsa, whose Pastor, Dr. Jon Wakefield, mobilized prayer for the healing of Dennis. He was a veteran missionary in Africa and has been a strong supporter of our mission work in Sri Lanka.

Our sons, Mark, Stephan and Dennis, have obviously been an integral part of our family, the church and the ministry, especially in Kandy. Mark conducted several Medical Clinics and promoted the Patmos Media (Film Ministry) in remote towns and villages. The Volksmission in Reutlingen, as well as friends in Germany, donated a brand new video

---

[2] Abbreviation of the city Udhagamandalam (also known as Ootacamund)

beamer to screen films in villages and tea plantations. Shortly after, they also donated a much needed van for the Film Ministry.

On one occasion, Mark and Stephan were on their way to Hiripitya in the Kurunegala area. They were to show the "Jesus Film". They were invited by Pastor David Gnanakan. They left our home at about six that evening and called us to say that they had a flat tire. They used the spare wheel, made it to the church, and showed the film. On their return, half-way to Kandy and on a deserted road, the spare gave out and they were left stranded. A passerby took them to a garage and managed to have it repaired. Both of them staggered into our home past midnight, totally exhausted. Their troubles were not in vain. Pastor David, even today, speaks of how the film was shown and how many people turned to the Lord because of it. Hiripitiya is a stronghold of satanic power and the spirits evidently resented those who were bringing the Gospel Light into this dark region.

Communication began with cave paintings, maps and writing. Cyrus, the Persian Emperor, is credited with having created the modern postal system when he conquered media. He implemented a network of Postal services to keep the Empire connected.

Electronic media has overtaken postal and print, and brought people living far and near together. Computers, mobile phones, e-mail, Facebook and Skype have revolutionized the way man communicates today. While the Christian message of the Gospel should be unchanged, the method of communication must be in keeping with the progress of information technology.

With this in mind, we embarked on screening Christian Films and also producing them. In 1974 we produced our first Christian movie with the help of Ken Anderson of Ken Anderson Films. It was called *"Elephant Boy."* It had a clear Christian theme and appealed to a young audience. The star was a young lad from Trinity College who acted as the "Elephant Boy".

I was its associate producer and wrote most of the story for the film. The narrator was George Beverly Shea the famous Soloist of the Billy Graham Crusades.

The entire cast was from Kandy, Sri Lanka, and most of the actors from the Lighthouse Church. The film has since been translated into Spanish.

The Patmos Ministry, under the leadership of Mark and Pastor Job, also known as Lanka Media Vision, was initiated, to reach the millions of lost people in the island with the soul saving Gospel message through films, videos and TV to spread the Good News.

The Patmos team took the Gospel through the media of films to schools, tea plantations, villages and churches. About 5,000 have already seen these films. The two major films being screened are the Campus Crusade film "Jesus" and the epic film "Man of Mercy" *(Karunamoorthy).* The 'Jesus' film had a cast of 5,000 and was filmed in Israel. The film is in Sinhala and can you imagine their amazement, as the people heard Jesus speak in their own language.

The *'Man of Mercy'* film was produced by Bollywood and runs for nearly three hours. It portrays the birth, baptism, ministry, trial, crucifixion and resurrection in vivid detail. People gasp and are moved to tears as they watch the nails being hammered into the palms of Jesus. The film is in Tamil and is with and all-Indian cast.

The films are a powerful tool to evangelise and also teach the Scripture. New believers are able to see on screen within a very short time, how Jesus lived, healed the sick, taught the disciples, died on the cross and how He rose again within a very short time on screen. For the unbeliever, the vivid portrayal of the crucifixion, drives home the truth, that Jesus sacrificed His life to save sinners.

After every showing, leaders of the churches and groups would appeal to us to come and show it in their own area, promising to do all publicity for the film. Mark and his team showed the film in a tea estate and around 500 people were present, including the police chief of that area. Many came forward to receive salvation and healing. Some of the local leaders wanted us to come and show the film in every plantation in the area. Usually each plantation had about 1,000 people working in them.

In 1999, a great opportunity opened up for the Patmos Ministry. The Cricket World Cup was held in London from the 13th of May to the 13th of June and fifteen countries, including England, Pakistan, India, Australia and Sri Lanka participated in the game. These matches would be watched by over one billion people the world over, and with Sri Lanka, being the reigning world champions at that time, ensured that all Sri Lankans were excited and awaiting the games to be telecast live on the television channel *Swarnavahini* from 7 – 11 pm each day.

It was here that a unique opportunity opened up for the Patmos Media Ministry. Mark told us that the PMM had booked thirty sites to show the cricket matches on our huge screen. We expected thousands to gather at these outdoor venues to view the match. During the breaks and lunch intervals in the game, we would screen the testimonies of Christian cricket stars who had been born again.

About 50,000 booklets titled *"Join the Winning Team"*, explaining the Gospel message, were distributed at these sites. Moreover, we chose to show the film in areas that were traditionally opposed to the Gospel. One such area was Narammala, where, in 1998, a church was burnt and the pastor had been assaulted.

Thousands of people had begun to pray for this outreach. Prayer, much needed for a team that worked day and night during the thirty days and also for the salvation of thousands of people.

The medical clinics began in the early 1970s with Dr. Chara. We treated hundreds upon hundreds of sick people free of charge and also gave them drugs and medication free of cost. After all, more people go through hospitals than through churches!

Our eldest son, Mark, when he returned from the USA, took over the responsibility of conducting these medical camps. In 1999, our youngest son, Dennis, on one of his visits, also held a medical camp in Pothupitiya and the doctors treated many sick patients.

On July 31st, 1999, we held our very first Hope Angel Medical Clinic in Pothupitiya which sits at the foothills of Alagalla Hill and is surrounded by jungle and tea land. People here either work in the tea estates or as day labourers. More than half of the men do not hold regular jobs. Many earn a very small amount which is barely enough for them to survive. In some families, both parents work, leaving the children in the care of aged grandparents. When they return home from a hard day's work they would beat a path to the nearest tavern where *'Kassipu'* or hard, home brewn liquor is illegally sold. Both men and women have become addicted to drink.

About three years earlier, we had built a church in this area with about fifty people attending services. These were first-generation Christians. There was very little medical help available for the scattered population. Parents had no money or inclination to take their sick children for treatment. Around this time we heard of two children that had died due to sheer neglect and it was in such an area that we conducted our Hope Angel Clinic.

The number we treated rose to 130 patients. Many came for help long after we had closed. We had to hire the doctor, the male nurse, and assistants were provided by the Pothupitiya church. Several of them helped in many ways. We found that many children suffered from scabies by playing in contaminated sand. Leeches abound here in plenty. One woman who came to the clinic had oozing in the ear for two years and had not sought treatment.

During the afternoon, a mother brought her child for treatment. The doctor took one look and told the mother to take the child to the main hospital or it may have a cardiac arrest. The young mother started weeping since getting to the hospital would take hours from that place. Immediately on hearing this, Hildegard and Mark bundled them into the van and raced to the nearest hospital with red lights flashing. Fortunately they arrived in time and the child was placed on a nebulizer and after treatment went back home.

The father of the child, who was also in the van that rushed his child to hospital, was a well-known temple dancer. He heard the prayers raised for his child by total strangers and we hope and pray that one day he would find the Christ who died for him.

On one occasion, Mark and Shania went to an estate in the Knuckles range. These are remote places where there are no hospitals and clinics. The nearest hospital was 10-15 miles away and transport is difficult. There was no proper school hall to hold the clinic. They decided to use an old barn used to collect paddy. People sat for hours to be diagnosed and treated. A large numbers of mothers and children attended these camps. A prayer was made before the start of the meeting and at the end a short message on how to be saved.

* * *

All three of our boys studied at Hebron International School in Ooty in Tamil Nadu, India, one of the oldest Missionary Schools founded by British Missionaries. They all excelled in Table Tennis and Swimming.

It was during the height of the JVP insurgency and the LTTE conflict that they travelled to Colombo to board a flight to India. Many times, on their return, they were stopped in the dead of night by Army personnel and questioned. There were reported occasions when the army had opened fire on vehicles in the night for not stopping, killing those inside.

Our family, Hildegard, Stephan and Dennis were returning to India. The annual vacation from Hebron School, where Stephan and Dennis were students, was over. Usually we flew into Trichy airport and then travelled to Ooty by rented car, which took 7-8 hours. The return journey also took about the same time. From Trichy we would fly to Colombo which was a 45 minutes plane ride.

Trichy is a city state in Tamil Nadu and famous for its Rock Fort and Hindu Temples. The city does not sleep, for, day and night, people, buses and trains arrive and depart from this city. The blaring of horns and the incessant din of vendors yelling out to attract buyers, goes on and on.

We arrived late one evening in Trichy and booked into a hotel for the night. Our flight on Indian Airlines was scheduled to depart at 10 am the next day. The morning of our departure, we showered and packed our bags and came down to the reception to clear our bills. While they prepared our bills our baggage was brought down by the room boy, and kept near the reception desk. The four of us had four small suitcases, and one red bag in which we had kept our passports and other valuable documents.

After making the payments, we went out to the rented taxi and the room boy followed us with our bags including the red bag, which we watched very carefully, and placed them inside the boot while we took our seats. Assuming that all the bags were inside the car, we told the driver to head to the airport. When we arrived at the airport we looked for the red bag to fetch our passports from and to our surprise, it was nowhere to be seen. Needless to say, some panic set in. The time now was 8.30 am and it was time to go through Customs and Immigration. Deciding to return to the Hotel, we rushed to the reception and asked the clerk whether he had seen a red bag. He firmly said "No, we have not seen that bag." After a desperate search to see whether it was lying around, we jumped back into the car and sped to the airport to check again whether we had misplaced it as we unloaded our bags. No sign of any red bag.

Suddenly, Hildegard said, "Let's go back to the hotel." It did not make any sense, since we had just been there and checked the reception area. On the way, we both were silently praying. Hildegard got off the taxi, and went to the reception, and told the clerk that she wanted to check the room in which we had stayed the night. The man gave us a key to room 215 and we rushed up the stairs and opened the door. To our great relief we saw the red bag placed near the bed. We grabbed it and rushed down, hopped into the taxi and raced as fast as we could to the airport.

What happened? The room boy did not put the red bag into the car, but had hidden it in a corner. As soon as we left, he had taken the bag upstairs. He then would look inside for valuables or money before discarding it. This often happens when tourists are leaving a hotel. If they are in a hurry to catch a flight and if there aren't any valuables, they may not take the trouble to come back for that one bag.

While seated safely inside the plane, I asked Hildegard how she knew the red bag was in the room. She said that as she prayed, she heard a voice saying, "Go back and look inside the room you occupied last night." We thanked the Lord for his Wonderful Grace that saved us from immense difficulty. If we had lost the passports it would have meant a trip to Chennai, to the German and Sri Lankan Embassies.

Furthermore we had already spent most of our money during our stay in Ooty and little was left over for more Hotel expanses and new tickets.

Ironically, the number of our room was 215 – '5' being the number of Grace! We got off the plane at the Colombo airport and walked thorough Immigration with our passports and on to Kandy, rejoicing in the Amazing Grace of God that saved us from great trouble.

* * *

All three of our sons, after High School, proceeded to the USA to pursue their studies. Mark went to University of Oklahoma, Stephan and Dennis to Oral Roberts University. Dennis came back to Sri Lanka for a short time and was about to get his Private Plane License when on the day he was ready for the final exam there was a bomb blast in Colombo and the Air Force cancelled all interior flights. Our sons, too, have been through critical and dangerous times when they went to school in Sri Lanka and India. Amazing Grace has protected them.

There is one incident worth mentioning as to how we began our Sky Media Recording studio. When Dennis was in Sri Lanka on holiday in 2004, he was keen to get a Satellite connection. The three of us, Dennis, Dilantha and myself, went to a well-guarded building in Ratmalana that was supposed to help with satellite connections. We cautiously walked in, disregarding the Security at the gates and walked right into the Chairman's room.

The Chairman, a broad-shouldered gentleman, sat behind a wide desk. We asked him if we could get a Satellite connection here for our television set to which he replied that they were not providers of such equipment, however they are a Television Station, broadcasting to many countries around the world. As it was just before Christmas, I asked him whether he would accept a Christmas Program for telecast. He said, "If you bring it before the 27th, we could do it for free."

Wow! That sounded fantastic. We promised to send the tape to him in a few days. We quickly called our musicians and vocalist and recorded a Christmas program with a message on why Jesus was born. The tape was accepted and telecast on the 30th, to a world-wide audience. This unexpected open door to Satellite Television and our ability to record a half hour program so quickly, set us on the road to establishing one of the first Christian Production Studio's in Sri Lanka.

In the Bible, there is a story of a man called Saul who set out to find his lost donkeys and ended by being installed as the King of Israel. We set out with Dennis to find a Satellite establishing link and ended up, by setting up Sky Media, which eventually aired programmes to many nations. Dennis had a business which began with the name Sky and we decided, that, would be a good name for our Studio – Sky Media.

21

The Tsunami of 2004. Stephan Arrives to Assist Tsunami Victims. An Out-of-Control Jeep and a Miraculous Save. Boat Building Company Formed. New Covenant Relocates to Wellawatte. The Bullet-Proof Pastor.

ON THAT FATEFUL DAY, THE 26TH OF DECEMBER, 2004, WE WERE AT A church in Frisco, Dallas, when Nirmal de Silva called us to report a huge wave had hit the coastal areas. The word 'Tsunami' was practically unheard of then. Evidently, an earthquake of a magnitude of 9 on the Richter scale occurred below the seafloor in the Indian Plate, raising the sea floor by four to five metres near Indonesia.

The huge tidal wave sped at 800 mph to the coastal regions of Thailand, India and Sri Lanka. Over 36,000 were killed in Sri Lanka alone, and five million lost their homes across all the countries that the Tsunami hit. A coastline train, the "*Queen of the Ocean*" left Colombo headed on its coastal route towards Galle. When it reached Telwatte (now called Peraliya[1]) a wave swallowed the beaches and the train track, and the train itself came to a sudden halt. People from the surrounding areas climbed atop the carriages, hoping to be safe from the waves. This proved to be a fatal move. The next wave picked up the wagon and smashed them against trees and houses, killing all who had sought refuge on the train. The carriage doors were open with the train being packed, and the water came rushing in, soon filling the carriages and drowning all inside. A total

[1] '*Peraliya*' literally means 'overturned'

of 1,700 people died in this one tragic incident that day.

A bus carrying thirty passengers was hit by the waves and started to rise and overturn in the rising waters. Two believers in the bus began to pray, audibly to save them. Other passengers, who were non-Christians, also joined in. The waves receded and the bus stabilized itself, the passengers stepped out thanking the two sisters and attributed their deliverance to the Lord Jesus Christ.

On hearing this dreadful news, our family, Mark and Shania, Stephan and Amy sent out urgent letters for help. We had a family meeting and Stephan volunteered to fly to Sri Lanka with two brothers from Dallas. We gave him money to buy some backpacks and he flew to Colombo where he was picked up by Anura Dharmakirti who was acting for us at the NCC.

The scale of devastation was hardly realized, since, with every new day, fresh reports were coming in of families, their homes destroyed, housed in schools or churches on the East coast without any food or even clothes.

Within 72 hours of the news of this massive catastrophe being heard, a group of Israeli doctors flew into the country. They were staying in a hotel as they had to obtain permission from the government to do medical work. Since Israel and Sri Lanka had no diplomatic relations, the Government was hesitant to give them permission to travel to these areas.

Stephan, when he arrived in Sri Lanka, sent us this account, which was reported in the *Hope for Asia* January 2005 newsletter:

> I arrived in Colombo on the 1st, spending New Year on an aircraft somewhere over Dubai. The next day we loaded two trucks packed full with clothes, dry rations and blankets. The journey was arduous, over potholed roads and circumnavigating stray elephants, and we finally managed to reach the eastern coast by 1.00 am. We bided our time till 3.00 am since we were afraid we would be mobbed and people would have forcibly taken everything away.
>
> On our way home, we made a detour and came across a camp, not set up by the government or the UN, but by the villagers. They told us that they had not eaten anything, and had not received rations as hardly a soul passed that way. Pastor Anura and I went back and brought a hundred dollars worth of rice, canned fish and other food items. It was now around three in the afternoon. By the time we returned, cooking fires were already

> lit and we were soon able to feed them. Their plight was so dire that even over this meal, they began to cry. Yes, we fed them today, but what about tomorrow and the day after?
>
> Later that evening, I walked towards the beach. I saw pots and pans and clothes scattered everywhere; no one had taken any of these. When I asked Anura why, his answer was grim, "This is a graveyard." I looked around and saw a small pair of pink baby shoes lying in the sand. I picked them up and could not help but wonder if the baby had made it or if she had been swept away. It was heartbreaking.

The Volksmission, Hildegard's home church in Reutlingen, soon became the centre from where aid poured in, directed and organised by our dear friends Klaus Henning and Christel Amman. They, along with the Pastor, Gerhard Kirschenmann, worked unceasingly.

Stephan and Anura returned back to Colombo. Stephan had fever and was advised to take rest, however he downed some antibiotics and went ahead anyway. Hildegard, was back in Colombo. The NCC believers worked in teams day and night, shopping, packing and loading another two truckloads with food and utensils. Since Israel had no diplomatic links with Sri Lanka the twelve Israelis were not permitted to get involved on their own in any aid work. However, the American Embassy told them to work with a church. One of our believers had met with them and they decided to fund the trucks and the medicine for the refugees. So the two trucks, along with the Israelis, travelled to Trinco and Batticaloa and delivered the goods.

Stephan had more to report on subsequent trips and the following are excerpts from the *Hope for Asia* report of January 7th 2005, twelve days after the Boxing Day Tsunami:

> We were returning from Batticaloa, on the eastern coast of Sri Lanka, to Colombo, late at night. Batticaloa had suffered a number of cyclones in the past but never a Tsunami, which swept thousands into the sea on that Sunday morning, the 26th of December, 2004.
>
> Our Jeep swerved around a corner, totally out of control, to avoid an oncoming vehicle. We started to spin and I realized we were about to go over the edge of the road. I had no idea how far the drop would be as we couldn't see anything in the pitch darkness. As we went over the edge I whispered a prayer.

The Jeep hit a tree as it dropped off the edge, gaining speed as it went down. It crashed through a few smaller trees and, about fifteen feet further down, hit a concrete electric lamp post which broke into two pieces. Smoke began to bellow from the radiator and one of our lights flickered in the darkness.

I looked around and asked if everyone was alright. At first there was no reply; then I heard voices saying they were okay. The brand new Jeep was totalled, but we all walked away alive from that crash with only a few minor bruises. We managed to climb back to the top of the road and hailed a bus which took us back to Colombo.

Our trip, besides the accident, was quite successful. We went with three trucks loaded with medicine that the Israeli doctors had given us. They were given to the doctors that were manning the emergency camp. The refugees were brought here and wounds were treated. Another truck went straight to Batticaloa where we rendezvoused at noon.

Our plan was to take this truck to a village deep within the district. We had heard that the only bridge to this village was washed away and no one was making their way to this village. We tried to make a detour, but our Jeep got stuck in the mud, forcing us to get out and push. We then sent a messenger on to the village, asking for them to come and collect the food and medicine we had brought which they gladly did, collecting the rations and taking it home to their families.

We then took the truck to another refugee camp controlled by the TRO (Tamil Relief Organisation, which was a front for the Tamil Tiger Liberation movement). This 'organisation' would give just twenty percent of the aid meant for the people and keep back the remaining eighty percent for their organisation. Nevertheless, our contact man made sure that all the aid went to the people. I was there to see it personally delivered to the refugees. Among the items were packets of milk and baby formula, cooking utensils, protein supplements and water purification tablets.

This village had some 1,400 people and nearly 250 children. They lived in abject poverty. Speaking to these refugees, we asked them to take us back to their own village. We drove for an hour along the beach as the road was washed away. Finally, we made it to a place that could have been described, under normal circumstances, a heaven on earth. The village was nestled between pine trees that grew alongside large coconut palms by the side of the beach. Behind the village was a lagoon. You could wake up on this eastern shore to watch the sun rise over the ocean and go to sleep at night as it sets over the lagoon waters.

I looked around and only saw the debris of houses torn down by the waves. Clothes were scattered everywhere. I walked through a shell of a house and on the floor I saw a photo album, a bottle, that was still full of baby milk, a birthday card and a driver's license; everything that belonged to the people who had died when the killer waves came rushing inland. The men with me began to cry. All I could do was put my arm around these men who were total strangers and weep with them.

These people needed to regain their livelihood. We needed to provide them with new boats so that they could go back to the sea to fish. I met with ten men who were heads of the village and laid out my plan for them. They all said that they were done with the sea and afraid to go back out to fish. These fishermen were tough people who would wake up at four o'clock every morning and risk their lives to catch fish to earn a living. They work hard and are a proud people. It really surprised me that they did not want to go back to the sea.

I then asked them what they would like to do and the response was some kind of business. After an hour of trying to narrow it down, I realized that in order to do what they wanted, they needed some kind of transportation and that they would prefer a bicycle to a boat. I chose five elders of the village to give me a list of everyone in the village who needed a bicycle.

Next we called the women and asked them what they wanted. They said they could build a *"kadai"* or a small store by the side of the street with a *cadjan* (coconut frond) roof and sell bread, nuts, and so on.

We were deeply saddened to hear of the Tsunami and the incredible suffering people had to undergo because of this natural disaster. The LTTE and JVP were man-made disasters and now the people, especially along the eastern coast, were bearing the brunt of those dreadful waves. Over 100,000 fisherman lost their fishing boats, nets and gear. Many of them watched as their loved ones were devoured by the murky waters. Some Tamil women, carried away into the sea, managed to clamber back to the beach. When they realized the waves had stripped them of their clothes, some jumped back into the sea and were drowned. They valued their modesty more than their life!

Hildegard and I had a strong urge to help these fishermen who had lost loved ones and boats; to help them get back to earning a living. We visited some of them and they told us how they were caught unawares and how they had suffered losses through this catastrophe.

As it was impossible to get any boats, we decided to build and donate canoes, as well as fibreglass boats with engines and nets, to these fisher folk who had lost everything. The response to our appeals was incredible. We built a boatyard in Palliyawatte, 20 miles off Colombo, on a land bordering the canal, river and sea; a perfect location for a boatyard. We called it the Deutsch Lanka Boatyard. Neville Fernando was appointed as the Manager of the Enterprise. Before these boats were handed over, we, or a Pastor from the South Coast or East Coast, gave a Gospel message and gave each of the beneficiaries a New Testament wrapped in polythene. Some of them found Christ and began to attend churches nearby.

Our medical mission, called Healing Hands, conducted free medical clinics along the coastal areas with Dr. Chara who came from Zambia to help us. We treated 18,000 Tsunami victims, some of them sick through consumption of water tainted with sulphuric acid. Almost all of them were given the Gospel, either orally or through literature.

The Volksmission in Reutlingen partnered with us to build these boats. A team from the UMC rushed to Sri Lanka and visited the Tsunami victims along the west coast, giving them clothes and packets of food. The New Creation Church, Singapore, sent a team to help us with the medical mission. All this Seaboard Mission was made possible by the prayer and giving of many who were deeply moved by the dreadful Tsunami.

* * *

In November 2007, the New Covenant Church moved from the Cargill's Food City building to the former Siloam Church building in E. S. Fernando Mawatha, Wellawatte. The NCC was now seven years old and we were looking for a permanent church building. According to some recent government legislation, the building of new churches was disallowed. The legislation permits renovation but not to erect a new structure. In view of this restriction and the whopping land prices we found it exceptionally difficult to find a suitable alternative to our present position. Prayer and intercession was the only way out.

At almost every prayer service, we began to bang on the doors of heaven in prayer. Then, one day, at the end of 2006, Kingsley called and said that the Siloam property was for sale. I asked him how much they were expecting and was taken aback when I heard the price: Rs. 30 million or nearly 300 lakhs! I told him that was beyond our income and assets. Kingsley replied, "You can if you have faith." For a second I thought, it is easy to talk faith but ground realities are different. We forgot about it.

At the beginning of 2007, he called again and said the Management was arriving from India and would make a decision as to whom they would sell it to. This news was dangerously serious. We now had to make a decision to negotiate with the Management or lose it forever. At their arrival Hildegard and I went and met them at the Siloam Guest House in Dehiwela. The Director said that they would love to sell it to a church, knowing that services would be continued there.

He said he would have to make a decision before 3 o'clock as there was another party keen to buy the property and re-build on it, but had asked the sellers to demolish the entire structure before the sale. The Director, Augustine, did not want to demolish the building as it was a Holy Place – a church.

Of course they wanted the full price of Rs. 23 million (€170.000) without any delay. As we negotiated, Augustine agreed to the offer to pay Rs. 2.5 million by the end February and a further Rs. 2.5 million by April with the balance over a period of sixteen months.

The next month we paid the management 2.5 million rupees as agreed. By the grace of God we were able to keep the appointed time for payments. Our believers gave jewellery, gold rings and even the keys to a car. When we sold all these, it came to exactly what we needed. On the same day and hour the last payment of 2.5 million had to be paid, a believer called and asked how much was necessary. I told him, "One million."

He told us to go and meet David in his office and start the signing procedures. "I will cash that amount right now at the bank and rush to the office." What a burden was lifted at this last moment. We thanked the Lord for his grace.

By now we received good news that the Pastor of Christliches Zentrum in Reutlingen. Pastor Gerhard Kirschenmann, who shared our vision for winning lost souls, and his Elders had joined us in fervent prayer for the purchase of the new building. He initiated the "World Mission" department of the church, which now has missions in several nations of the world. Above all, we are grateful to the Christliches Zentrum and its leaders for their faithful prayers for us and for Sri Lanka. Pastor Kirschenmann, with the agreement of the elders, was able to organise a loan for the full payment of the church, and by the end of September 2007, we settled our outstanding balance with the Siloam owners and the deed was transferred to us.

Now we had to travel to Germany and raise the money for the loan given to us from the Headquarters of the Mission. On the 29th of June 2009, on Hildegard's birthday, Christel Amman called, wishing Hildegard on her birthday and continuing with the wonderful news. The Headquarters had received the full amount we had to pay back. Churches, families and individuals gave generously and we were debt free! We still continue to thank the Lord to have our own church building as the government has not given permission to build new churches. In the meantime, sadly, many home churches had to close their doors.

The church is situated down E. S. Fernando Mawatha, a side road off the main Galle Road in Wellawatte. It is a postal zone of Colombo bearing no 6. Wellawatte is a densely populated part of Colombo. During the thirty-year war with the Tamil Tigers, thousands of Tamils fled the northern areas of Sri Lanka especially from Jaffna and the Wanni areas where fighting was concentrated. These were the perpetual War Zones where thousands were killed and property destroyed. Even the children of Pastor Pillai were brought to Colombo for studies as schools were destroyed and the Tigers kidnapped men and forced them to join the forces. Pillai and his wife stayed back in Kilinochchi and looked after the eighteen churches he had established. Brother Pillai was one of the converts of our 1972 Jaffna crusade. He stood with all his people, caring for them, visiting them in the bunkers, burying sometimes several members of one family who were killed by falling shells. He was known as the "Bullet Proof Pastor".

To accommodate thousands of families who flooded into Wellawatte, eighteen high-rise apartments were built over a period of about 20-25 years. Most of these apartments are occupied by Tamil families. Their children are the Tamil Diaspora now living in Europe and Canada. They remit a substantial amount of money to support the parents and relatives.

The New Covenant Church has a Tamil service every Sunday early in the morning. Tamil people are early risers and the meeting starts at 7.30 am. The Pastor of the Tamil Service is Nathan. He was a professional tailor who used to tailor attires for one of the former Presidents. Nathan was born a Hindu and was raised in an up-country tea plantation. He became an alcoholic and gradually became violent, especially after taking liquor. The particular kind of crude liquor, is brewed with native preparations that induce fierce behaviour.

When he returned from work, his children would hide under their beds, not knowing how he would behave that evening. They tried all means to cure him but failed. Finally in desperation, they had invited a Pastor from the village to come and pray for him. When the Pastor and assistant came to the house they had politely told him that the purpose of their visit was to pray for him. He had agreed and before they could even kneel down, Nathan had asked them where the statue of their God was. The pastor replied, "We do not believe in making images or statues since it is forbidden in the Bible and anyhow, we cannot capture the form of God in wood, stone or clay."

At this reply, Nathan was furious and had told them both to get out of the house immediately. (Venerating and deifying natural forces and animals are readily accepted by Hindus). When his personal conditions began to deteriorate, he finally agreed to let them come back and pray for him.

The Pastor and assistant returned and prayed for him and cast out evil spirits that had been tormenting him for many years. He repented, received Christ as Saviour, was baptized and filled with the Holy Spirit. He now serves as the Shepherd, Preacher, Teacher and mentor to many youths in the Tamil Congregation. Nathan has turned out to be one of the most patient, caring and loving men on our staff at NCC.

We built our own baptismal tank under the podium of the NCC and have conducted five Baptismal services for new converts. The church hall is now used to record TV messages, it is practically sound proof and the news that Jesus saves is proclaimed to nations from this location.

We are also, by word, literature and films, endeavouring to share the Saving Message of Jesus to the displaced, due to the War in the North and East. Many who were cast out of their homes and lands due to the long War have experienced the Abundant Grace of our Lord, by coming to Wellawatte.

22

The Inimitable Pastor Philip. Pastor Mathew and the Negombo Crusade. The Rainbow of the Covenant. The Negombo Charismatic Centre.

NEGOMBO WAS TRADITIONALLY A FISHING VILLAGE LOCATED A few miles north up the coast from Colombo, with wide sandy beaches. Today, it is a developing and vibrant city with tourist hotels and Free Trade Zones. The Dutch captured it from the Portuguese in 1640 and the British captured it from the Dutch in 1796. The name 'Negombo' is a corruption of the word *Meegamuwa* from the Sinhala. According to legend, the squad of King Kavantissa found bee's honey in a canoe and it was brought to Viharamahadevi when she was pregnant. '*Mee*' translates to honey in Sinhala.

Negombo is a multi-religious city, with twenty Roman Catholic churches, some of them with large parishes. Due to the presence of a large number of Roman Catholic churches, Negombo is also called "Little Rome". However, today, there are over thirty Full Gospel churches in Negombo.

My elder brother, M. C. Mathew, re-located to Negombo from Calvary Church, Colombo, with a vision to establish a Full Gospel Church in the city. He and his wife Chrisanthie and son Johnny came back from England and started to work here.

Chrisanthie was the daughter of Pastor Phillip, a man you would never forget once you met him. He was tall with long, flowing white hair and a well-trimmed white beard. He had strong Aryan features and looked every inch like one of the prophets depicted in the Bible. He wore national dress but spoke impeccable English and his diction was unbeatable. He would preach for two to three hours on the Cross of Christ and travelled widely, preaching in conventions throughout India. He, I suspect, was inspired by Sadhu Sundar Singh of India and modelled his physical appearance and ministry like the Sahdu. People were fascinated by his appearance, as he looked as if he had stepped out of a time machine from Bible times.

Pastor Philip often spoke at our churches. On one occasion, he preached at an open air service in the town of Galle. A brother interpreted what he said into Sinhala, however a Swedish brother, standing next to me, would frequently ask me what Pastor Philip was saying as he could not understand his lofty English! I doubt whether anyone else in the crowd understood what he was saying either.

My brother Mathew was a graduate of the Birmingham Bible College and was a resilient personality. He could weather any storms. He was part of the founding members of the Fellowship of Free Churches which included Tissa, Ranjit, Hugh, Mathew, Krishnarajah and I. He, along with my younger brother, has baptized thousands of converts over the past decades.

In 1977, we decided to hold a Mass Healing Crusade in Negombo. At that time, there was just one Full Gospel 'Faith Home' in the area. The rest were Roman Catholic and Mainline or historic churches. The Crusade was to be held on the Esplanade close to the sea. Thousands of handbills were distributed and posters plastered on walls and notice boards. The reception to this was not all good with some of these handbills torn and strewn on the streets and posters also defaced.

We travelled frequently from Kandy to supervise the campaign and on one occasion while we were driving to Mathew's home along the main Negombo Road, we stopped at a gas station. While the attendee was pumping gas, I said a silent prayer, *'Lord, if this is your will that we should come and hold the crusade here, please show me a sign now.'* I looked up and out of my window and saw a perfectly formed and beautiful rainbow in the clouds. I knew that was it. The Lord, who made a covenant with us, had confirmed that He would be with us in Negombo.

The meeting commenced with about 1,000 people and on the very first night a Moslem lady who was deaf was healed and could hear sounds again. The next day, the crowds doubled and kept on increasing daily.

One night, as the crusade was going on, Christopher, a young man, came to the Crusade ground. He was suffering from a stomach ailment, was severely depressed and had decided to take his life. He carried a pistol and had two bullets in his pocket. To make sure that the gun was working properly, he shot a pig that was roaming in the area. While he was walking towards the beach to shoot the remaining bullet into his head, he heard the sound of music coming from the beach area. Curious as to what was going on, he came and stood at the back of the crowd. After the altar call was given, prayer was made en masse, and the power of God knocked him down and he was delivered from every bondage and oppression. When he rose from the ground he was a new man – born again. Christopher was baptized in water and in the Holy Spirit and became a full time servant of the Lord. Since then, he has capably interpreted my messages for many years.

On the last day there were around seven to eight thousand people. To this day, people still call it the "Main Crusade" that was conducted in Negombo.

The Crusade was now over and hundreds of new believers had to be discipled and taught the Word of God. It was a struggle for Pastor Mathew to raise the funds to purchase a plot of land and also build a Sanctuary that would seat 500 people. He had managed to raise part of the money to buy a property in the heart of the town and had made a down payment. The deadline for final payment to acquire the property was fast approaching and there was no sign of any funds coming in. A week before the deadline, Rudy Schwabe (Hildegard's brother) came with a team from his Church in Germany and was prompted to give a substantial amount of money towards the project. Pastor Mathew later informed us that he was able to make the final payment with the donation given by Rudy three days before the deadline.

23

The Founding of the Volksmission. The Awakening German Church. Volksmission Churches. Healings and Prayer Seminar in Ridnu Valley. Miracle of the Twins. German Pastors and Believers visit Sri Lanka, Bringing Hope to the People.

OVER THE PAST FORTY YEARS, A LARGE PART OF OUR MEETINGS were held within the Volksmission Churches of Germany. We conducted Crusades and Prayer Seminars in churches, city halls and in tents. The annual convention of the Volksmission attracts close to 1,000 believers. I have had the privilege of speaking there on two occasions with Hildegard by my side both as my interpreter and prayer partner.

The Volksmission was founded by Karl Fix during Germany's most traumatic years. Bravely standing up to the likes of Hitler and the Gestapo, Fix conducted open air services, despite the ban on public meetings, and distributed two million tracts over twelve countries.

In 1946, he baptized 250 people, which saw the beginning of the Volksmission. Karl Fix passed away on the 19th of January, 1969. I was present at his funeral and had only a faint idea at that time of the man and his accomplishments in Germany through his courage and faith.[1]

Today the Volksmission has grown to over seventy churches in southern Germany with missionaries serving in many nations.

When I first visited the Volksmission in the late nineteen sixties, the

[1] *Ref:* B. Rockle (2003) *"Born in Difficult Times. Founder of the Volksmission - Karl Fix"* Glyndwr University

services were held in houses converted to accommodate 50-70 people. The songs were sung from a hymn book called *"Pfingst Jubel"* and the proceedings were predictable. By the late seventies and early eighties, overheads replaced the Hymn books. Scripture choruses were widely used which attracted the youth. By the beginning of the end of the 80s congregations were building their own Sanctuaries, which were able to hold 300-400 people. A few could accommodate around 1,000 people. The permanent church buildings encouraged more people to attend the services and become members.

Invitations began to arrive at our desk from many Pastors in Germany, to hold seminars and crusades.

In April 1994, we conducted a ten day Prayer Seminar for German believers in Ridnu Valley in northern Italy.[2] I spoke for sixteen hours during this seminar with Hildegard ably interpreting the messages. People began to pray more intensively and aggressively for lost souls and for the breaking of strongholds. Michael from Rumania broke down and wept. He gave his heart to the Lord, rising up with his face shining. Whenever we visit the Reutlingen Church, he hurries to come and embrace me.

During our frequent visits and meetings, many were miraculously healed by the power of God. We conducted a series of meetings in Sulz in the Black Forest area and this is what we reported in our Sri Lankan Newsletter of October 1990.

> "At the end of the first day, Wilhelm Faust, a member of the church came and thanked us for praying for him during our crusade in August 1988. He said. "In 1988, I had seven operations to remove a tumourous cancer; cancer cells had formed into a large tumour, and caused several structural changes in my body. During the crusade, I prayed for healing. I was later checked by the Professor of Nuclear Medicine, Dr. Drescher, and my condition was clear. Again, this year, February 1990, I underwent a medical test and all the tests were negative. Praise God for His healing power!"

At another service held at a church in Pluderhausen, a small town near Stuttgart, a young couple were seated in the back row, their face radiant and smiling at us throughout the meeting. We found ourselves wondering what could make them so extremely happy. At the end of the service

[2] *Ref: Sri Lanka Newsletter* – August 1994

they approached us and showed us pictures of the little twin daughters. Hildegard mentioned how sweet they looked. They then reminded us, "My wife and I had been married for four years and did not have any children. We asked you last year to pray for a child and after prayer, you asked us to show us our baby when you came back." We looked over and over at the photo as they said, "God blessed us in a wonderful way; we had not just one baby, but twins! Thank you for your prayers."

Our Evangelistic meetings in German churches were greatly appreciated. The services in churches and halls usually lasted for several hours as the Holy Spirit began to move upon the people with the gifts of healing and revelation. On one occasion, we had a meeting near the East German Border and were somewhat disappointed, since there were only three ladies present. At the end of the service one lady told us she gave her heart to Christ, another testified that she was healed and the third person was praising the Lord for baptizing her with the Holy Spirit. This was the only time we had one hundred percent "success" in the ministry.

On our many returns to Sri Lanka after crusades, many Pastors and believers began to pray for Sri Lanka, as we were now in the midst of the Liberation Tiger War. The LTTE was at its pinnacle of power and they had now grabbed a large swath of territory in the northern part of the island.

Due to the frequent bombings of the cities in the South by the Tigers, visitors to churches from abroad became a trickle. However, we were deeply thankful to Pastors and believers who braved these dreadful conditions and came to minister and encourage the churches. Among them was Karl Schock from Shorndorf, the town where Daimler Benz produced the world famous Benz cars. We preached often at Scala, the church founded by Karl Schock, which is one of the largest churches in the Volksmission. Karl taught at the Lanka Bible College and Karl with his wife Helga were the main speakers when we dedicated the New Life Church in Kurunegala.

Gotlob Ling, Ernst Goehner and Werner Fraas visited and preached in different churches. Many responded to the altar calls during their meetings. Albert Kepler had special meetings in Kegalle seeing the church crowded with people seeking prayer. One man who was deformed in his right hand was immediately healed and others were filled with the Spirit.

Dietmar Schwabe came to Sri Lanka when he was eighteen years old. On his vacation, he lived with us for six months and was well-received by the students of the Bible College. They travelled to the hill country and preached the Gospel in the villages and towns. When he returned to Germany, he became a Youth Leader in Reutlingen and then on to Bible College. After graduation, he became a Pastor of the Volksmission in Klosterreichenback. Today, he is one of the lecturers of the Beroa Bible College in Erzhausen.

Christel Amman and Klaus Henning, who head the "Freundeskreis" Sri Lanka Mission, formed the Friends of Sri Lanka Mission to mobilize prayer partners in the German Churches. They prepared and organized our meetings and passed on information to the German churches. Both Klaus and Christel have a passion for souls and have tirelessly worked to extend the Kingdom here in Sri Lanka. They have been assisting us in the many different ministries and projects with professional aptitude and Christ-like compassion. Both of them came to Sri Lanka and visited many churches.

When we dedicated the Church in Pothupitiya, Christel was shown a vision of a bright light spreading rapidly in all directions of the island. As the Body of Christ from the East and West joined in prayer and work, the people who sat in darkness have seen a great light, the Light of the Gospel of Jesus Christ.

24

The Asian Quest for the Supernatural. The Maha Kumba Mela – A Silhouette of the Festival. The Naga Sadhus or Holy Men. Ten Thousand New Sadhus Integrated. The Biblical Response.

THE MAHA KUMBA MELA FESTIVAL IS HELD EVERY TWELVE YEARS on the banks of the River Ganges. Every twelve years, between 80-100 million people will gather along its banks to dip or bathe in its waters. This is considered the largest festival in the history of the world. The last festival began this year (2013) in January.

This river flows from the snowy mountains of the Himalaya across the plains of the northern region of the Ganges and empty itself into the Bay of Bengal. According to the Hindus, this river descended from heaven and is the vehicle of ascent into heaven. Those who bathe in its waters are promised instant Salvation. This sacred river is considered to be pure and to purify the soul.

The major event is the ritual bathing of saffron clad Sadhus who come to this festival buffed in ash and powder. The saffron robe is a symbol of fire that has burnt all their earthly affections and desires. Thousands of them emerge from the caves of the Himalaya mountain region to ensure that they are able to dip or bathe in the river.

Among them are the *Naga Saniyasini* (Holy men) who wander around the banks – naked except for the ash rubbed on their bodies. These men, during the festival, live in temporary tents and show their prowess to the thronging pilgrims of all ages and ethnicity. Some of them can be seen inside these tents with gnarled upraised hand and nails protruding out of the fingers. Some of them have been holding their hands in this position for ten years. Others can be seen standing on one leg with the other leg cradled on the knee. Pilgrims seek them out to receive a blessing. It is not unusual for pilgrims to witness other *Naga Sanniyasini* lifting bricks weighing fifteen kilos with their manhood. After their performance, which is public, pilgrims scramble to be touched by them.

A day before the end of the Festival, the *Naga Sanyasini* will conduct mass classes for those who are now preparing to join the group. Thousands of them gather and are given instruction of how and what rituals are to be followed before being accepted into the camp. One ritual is for all of them to go into a special cubicle and have all their hair shaved. There are hundreds of such booths where barbers are waiting to cut their hair. Next day, thousands of these bald men, teenagers, old men with withered faces, and middle aged men with robust bodies will run to the river side to dip themselves in its waters. It is estimated that at every festival ten thousand men will be conscripted to their ranks!

They will now leave the banks of the river and seek caves in the Himalayas or wander as a "holy men" across the land.

While the mammoth sacrifices these men make to achieve *"moksha"* and Heaven, do they realize that their Ganges is considered to be the most polluted river in the world? Some 400 million people live in the basin of this river; the most densely populated real estate in the world. There are 1,000 inhabitants per square mile. The river contains eighty percent faecal and industrial matter and then it is emptied into the Bay of Bengal.

There are no simple answers as to why men, created in God's image, are ready to undergo inhuman pain and suffering to obtain an improbable and uncertain end. The Bible answer is that men are blinded by Satanic power and believe in delusions of the Evil One.

Romans Chapter One, verses 23 to 25 states: "what happened was this: people knew God perfectly well and when they didn't treat him like God refusing to worship him, they trivialized themselves into silliness and confusion so that there was no sense or direction to their lives. They traded the glory of God into… cheap figurines you can make and buy at any roadside." *(The Message: Eugene Peterson).*

Ephesians Chapter 4:17, "This I say and testify in the Lord that you walk not as other Gentiles walk in the vanity of their minds, having their understanding darkened, being alienated from the life of God thorough ignorance because of the blindness of their hearts."

"The Good news is that God took our sin-laden lives and made us alive in Christ. He has set us down in the highest Heaven in company with Christ our Messiah." *(Ephesians 2:4, 5 - The Message, Eugene Peterson)*

The mandate given to the church is to deliver this Good News that the Lord Jesus, on the cross, took our sin-laden lives and made us to sit in the Heavenly Places with Christ. Forgiveness of sin, peace with God, and the Peace of God is available through faith in Jesus Christ and his death and resurrection.

Bethesda Gospel Hall, Colombo

Bethesda Youth at Camp

My father, M. M. Chandy, my brother, M.C. Mathew, and my mother, Elizebeth Chandy.

From left to right - My Mother, Mathew, Jacob (seated) Roshan, Me and Libertus (standing)

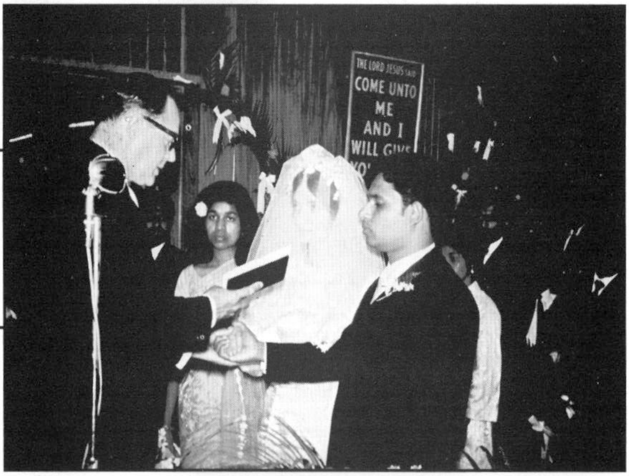

Our Wedding, Calvary Church, 24th February 1971

Travelling as an Evangelist in the USA in 1969

In Helsinki

In Germany

In the USA

With Dieter Kemesi in Germany

IBTI Practical work with Prabudas Vasu

Crusade Poster, Allen, Germany

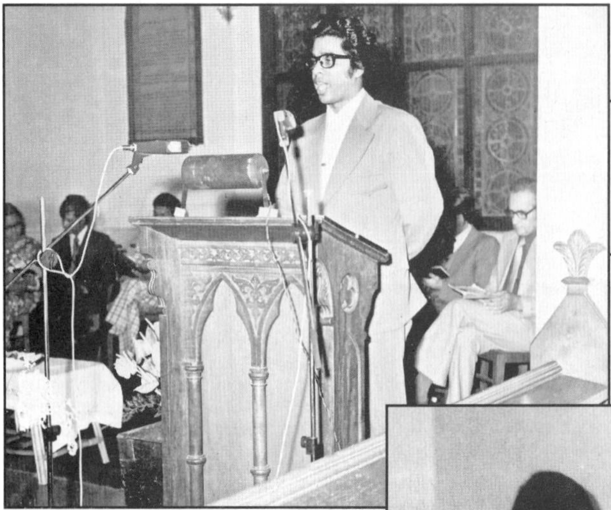

Dr. Tissa Weerasinghe at the LBC Graduation Service

LBC Graduation Service, Kandy

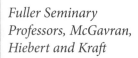

Fuller Seminary Professors, McGavran, Hiebert and Kraft

LBC Graduation, BMICH, Colombo

With Bertil Steffansson

Kandy Mass Crusade, 1978

Kandy Crusade

Voice of the Age at Jaffna Crusade

With Alexi and Nithi, Kandy Crusade

Winners' Camp, Kandy

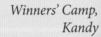

IPC Convention, Kerala

Lighthouse Church, Kandy

Bethlehem Church, Chilaw

Lighthouse Church, Gampola

With Rudy Schwabe, Germany

Hildegard at Church Dedication

Hildegard at NCC Dedication

New Covenant Church

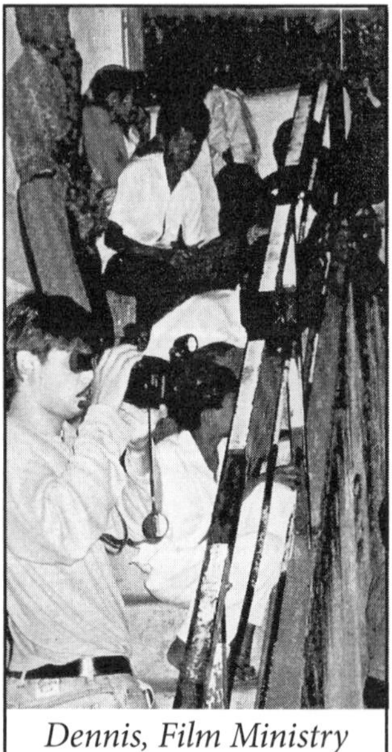

Dennis, Film Ministry

Stephan, Me, Hilde, Dennis and Mark

Mark and Shania, Mobile Clinic, 1999

Stephan and Donny, Tsunami Relief, 2005

Tsunami Relief, East Coast

Deutsch Lanka Boat Yard, Colombo

Studio, Sky Media International

'Miracle Service' TV Programme

INDEX

About the Author

Dr. Verghese Chandy earned a doctorate from the Fuller Theologcal Seminary in Pasadena, California in 1984.

Dr. Chandy is the founding President of the Lanka Bible College in Kandy.

He served as the Senior Lighthouse Church Pastor in Kandy for 17 years and as the Senior Pastor of the New Covenant Church in Colombo for 13 years.

He and his wife Hildegard Chandy have conducted city-wide crusades in India, Germany and Africa, reaching multitudes with the Gospel.

Pastor and Hildegard Chandy are the founders of the Healing Hands, and the Lanka Deutch Boat Company.

He is presently serving as the Vice-President of the Fellowship of Free Churches of Sri Lanka.

If you wish to contact the author
about the book, please email him at:

www.hopeforasia.org

or email:

warandgraceinfo@gmail.com

or

joyvision@hotmail.com

He will appreciate hearing from you